Fat Girl

Fat Girl

A True Story

Judith Moore

P
PROFILE BOOKS

First published in Great Britain in 2005 by
Profile Books Ltd
3A Exmouth House
Pine Street
London EC1R 0JH
www.profilebooks.com

First published in the United States in 2004 by
Hudson Street Press

"Reason for Music," from *Collected Poems of 1917–1982* by Archibald
MacLeish. Copyright © 1985 by the Estate of Archibald MacLeish.
Reprinted by permission of Houghton Mifflin Company. All rights reserved.

10 9 8 7 6 5 4 3 2 1

Printed and bound in Great Britain by
Clays, Bungay, Suffolk

A CIP catalogue record for this book is available from the British Library.

ISBN 1 86197 980 0

For Steven Barclay

"All this happened, more or less."

—Kurt Vonnegut Jr.,
Slaughterhouse Five

For their encouragement and assistance I am
grateful to the National Endowment for the Arts and
to the John Solomon Guggenheim Foundation.

I am fat. I am not so fat that I can't fasten the seat belt on the plane. But, fat I am. I wanted to write about what it was and is like for me, being fat.

This will not be a book about how I had an eating disorder and how I conquered this disorder through therapies or group process or antidepressants or religion or twelve-step programs or a personal trainer or white-knuckling it or the love of a good man (or woman). This will be the last time in this book you will see the words "eating disorder."

I am not a fat activist. This is not about the need for acceptance of fat people, although I would prefer that thinner people not find me disgusting.

I know, from being thin and listening to thin people talk about fat people, that thin people often denigrate fat people. At best, they feel sorry for them. I know too that when a thin person looks at a fat person, the thin person considers the fat person less virtuous than he. The fat person lacks willpower, pride, this wretched attitude,

Fat Girl

"self-esteem," and does not care about friends or family because if he or she did care about friends or family, he or she would not wander the earth looking like a repulsive sow, rhinoceros, hippo, elephant, general wide-mawed flesh-flopping flabby monster.

I will not write here about fat people I have known and I will not interview fat people. All I will do here is tell my story. I will not supply windbag notions about what's wrong with me. You will figure that out. I will tell you only what I know about myself, which is not all that much.

I will tell the story of my family and the food we ate. We were an unhappy family. With the exception of my father's maternal grandparents and a woman who worked for them and my adorable and generous gay uncle, nobody much loved anybody. Everybody was pretty much in it for themselves. We were hard American isolatos. We were solitaries. Unhappy families, though, still have to eat. For my father and for me, who are this story's primary fatsos, food was the source of some of our greatest pleasure and most terrible pain.

Narrators of first-person claptrap like this often greet the reader at the door with moist hugs and complaisant kisses. I won't. I will not endear myself. I won't put on airs. I am not that pleasant. The older I get the less pleasant I am.

I mistrust real-life stories that conclude on a triumphant note. Rockettes will not arrive on the final page and kick up their high heels and show petticoats. This is a story about an unhappy fat girl who became a fat woman who was happy and unhappy.

But I haven't always been fat. I had days when I was almost thin.

one

"Even sad stories are company.
And perhaps that's why you might read
such a chronicle, to look into a
companionable darkness that isn't yours."

—Mark Doty,
Firebird

"You're too fat to fuck."

I was eating dinner in a café with a fellow I liked. I shouldn't have liked him but I did. The café had been around for years and was popular and noisy. We were seated across from each other in a red Naugahyde booth.

I was eating a cheeseburger, holding the assemblage in both hands. Crisp around the edges, the bun was warm and squishy, squeezed between fingers and thumbs. It had been fried on the griddle, had soaked up meat grease, and my hands were getting greasy.

Fat Girl

I was glad that the meat and bun and cheese and lettuce and dill pickle and mustard and mayonnaise and chopped onion were inside my mouth. I was glad that I was chewing and that my mouth was full. The chewing and the taste of the cheeseburger mush that I pushed against the roof of my mouth with my tongue made me dreamy and forgetful.

I wanted to forget. I wanted to forget what the fellow sitting across from me had just said. He was drunk when he said it, but still, he said it and he meant it.

That was the last cheeseburger I ate. Now, fifteen years later, when I can't sleep, I conjure cheeseburgers. I summon the moist and porous bun, melted cheddar, a beef patty cooked rare, cool serrated dill pickle slices, chopped crisp lettuce, sharp grainy mustard and slicks of mayonnaise. I make and remake the cheeseburger; I pile on more pickle, add Spanish onion rings, add paper-thin tomato, and turn the bun greasier. The warm edge of slightly scratchy toasted bun, dense meat, melted cheese and the lettuce rest on my tongue. I sink back into my heaped pillows and fill a red plastic basket with onion rings. Not the trashy frozen onion rings coated in cornmeal. These onion rings are cloaked in tempura batter and plunged into roiling fat and pulled out when the batter turns gold. I dip the rings in tartar sauce, the cheap kind that comes in a jar.

Eventually, I fall off to sleep.

*   *   *

6

I am on a diet. I am almost always on a diet. I am try-ing to get rid of pounds of my waddling self. I am always trying to get rid of pounds of myself.

I am a short, squat toad of a woman. My curly auburn hair is fading. Curls form a clown's ruff about my round face. My shoulders are wide. My upper arms are as big as those maroon-skinned bolognas that hang from butchers' ceilings. My belly juts out. The skin on my thighs is pocked, not unlike worn foam rubber. When I walk my buttocks grind like the turbines I once saw move water over the top of Grand Coulee Dam.

My face looks not quite finished, as if the person who made it was in a hurry to get home from work and watch television news. I have pig eyes, with Mongoloid flaps. Now that I'm older my eyelids fall down over my blue-green eyes, giving me a sleepy, sullen appearance. My eyelashes are stubby. The pores of the skin on the flanges of my nose are enlarged. I have a thick lower lip. I have bad teeth. But mostly I am fat.

I hate myself. I have almost always hated myself. I have good reasons for hating myself, but it's not for bad things I've done. I do not hate myself for betrayals, for going behind the back of someone who trusted me. I hate myself because I am not beautiful. I hate myself because I am fat.

Everybody fat has her own fat story. There are dif-ferent ways fat folks get fat and lose fat and stay fat. Ninety percent of fat people who lose weight regain the lost fat within two years. So many fat people seem helpless against fat. I am one of them. (Maybe you are too? Or perhaps you are a long-limbed sylph who does not give Fritos and bean dip a thought?) I so effortlessly put on poundage that gain seems a form of magic. Four, five pounds a week, I can add. Abracadabra. Simply to gaze at a magazine photograph of, say, pineapple upside-down cake, and to read the accompanying recipe— pineapple rings, maraschino cherries, coconut, butter, brown sugar, eggs, cake flour, white sugar—add a jiggle to my wide hips.

Some fat women (and men) eat breakfasts that fairy-tale giants might eat—six sunny-side-up eggs, thick bacon slices and spicy sausage patties, hash brown potatoes, pancakes and butter and puffy French toast and maple syrup and fresh-squeezed orange juice and homogenized milk. For dinner they eat two-pound porterhouse steaks and an Idaho baked potato lavished with butter, sour cream, crumbled bacon and chives. They pop into the factory of their hardworking mouths crisp romaine leaves drenched in blue cheese dressing. They masticate celestially soft dinner rolls soaked in butter. They devour marbled cheesecake. Between meals, they snack on pizza from a corner pizzeria, on Baby Ruths and glazed doughnuts and maple bars and salty plump cashews and chocolate-coated ice cream bars and peanut butter cookies. They swill sugared soft drinks.

They weigh two hundred pounds and three hundred pounds and four hundred pounds and still they are hungry.

Some fat women (and men) lose extra poundage and keep it off. Others eat and vomit. Some take laxatives. Some binge—eat pounds of food at a sitting. Then they upchuck. I have never lugged home sacks of food and binged. I have never taken diet pills or made an appointment with a quack diet doctor. Nor have I gone the vomit or laxative route. Reverse peristalsis terrifies me and I don't like stomach cramps. I am a simple overeater. I am what nutritionists call a "yo-yo dieter." I gain twenty pounds and lose fifteen. I gain forty and lose fifty.

But not everyone is like me. Some people binge and then, for days, they starve. Some add exercise to starvation and run miles and spend evenings at a gym. Some fat girls become anorexic women. Some anorexic women die of starvation.

The world is full of thin women who behind flat stomachs shelter fat girls. Some thin women are thin for only a few weeks before they begin to get fat again. You can tell who those thin women are who give refuge to a fat girl. When they see the buffet table they square their shoulders. They ready for combat with Virginia baked ham, sweet potato soufflé and those puffy dinner rolls with butter and a three-layer chocolate mousse cake.

Food is the enemy.

Food also is the mother, the father, the warm-hearted lover, the house built of red brick that not even the wolf can blow down.

Some people daydream heroic deeds or sex scenes

or tropical vacations. I daydream crab legs dipped in hot butter or crab cakes dribbled with garlic aioli. I consider toasted cheese sandwiches or homemade lemonade pinkened with macerated strawberries or carrot cake with brown sugar frosting that I ate, once, twenty years ago, or, those cheeseburgers. Foods I ate once and liked I think about the way people think about old lovers. I entertain memories of clam strips and tartar sauce and cole slaw from an outdoor food stand in Maine or an ice cream flavor—Honey Vanilla—that Häagen-Dazs used to make. For thirty minutes I think about Honey Vanilla. Why did Häagen-Dazs quit making Honey Vanilla and what can I do to get them to make it again?

Aged English or New York cheddar, even tightly cosseted as it is in cheesecloth and tucked into the far back of the refrigerator's butter drawer, sings love songs in my ear. The cheddar croons about Braeburn apples in the fruit basket and round brown hazelnuts in the top drawer. Down the street an old-time bakery makes plain, unfashionable and not all that tasty pies. The filling for these pies comes from commercial-sized cans and the crusts are premade. These pies, from three blocks away, call, "Judith, Judith." An unopened bag of potato chips or an unopened box of vanilla wafers can sit in my pantry for months. I need exercise no self-control not to open these bags and boxes. However, once I open the containers, I can't quit eating. I want every chip, all the wafers. I do not know why this is.

I don't hunger after only high-calorie foods. I get hankerings for green beans, lettuces, red and yellow beets, crookneck squash, zucchini, tomatoes of all kinds, long burpless English cucumbers, celery and bell peppers. I long for Bosc pears, berries, peaches and plums and cherries and nectarines and figs both white and brown. I am mad for fresh-squeezed tangerine juice. I crave certain summer melons—orange-flesh honeydew, the Galia (with webbed cantaloupe-like skin and pale green honeydew-like flesh) and plain old cantaloupe the way my bestial maternal grandmother did it. What she did was peel and seed and cut melon into thin wedges—Rocky Ford was her melon of choice—and pack the wedges into a clean wide-mouthed Kerr canning jar. She stored the melon-filled jar in the refrigerator and you could reach in and take out the cold jar, unscrew the lid, pull out a melon wedge and suck it into your hot, dry mouth. The melon's chilly flesh collapsed across your tongue.

Not long ago on a summer afternoon when the temperature outside was over one hundred degrees I opened the refrigerator. Cool air drifted out onto my hands and arms. The light that gilded the shelves was not all that different from lights that hang over Old Masters in museums. Earlier that day I had used the melon baller and made melon balls from the flesh of a Sugar Baby. I popped one of the watermelon balls into my hot mouth. I sucked pale red flesh away from black seeds. I turned and spit seeds into the sink.

I've rarely eaten fast foods. Thirty years have passed since I ate anything from McDonald's. I've never walked through the door of one of these chain restaurants that I see advertised on television. That said, I

Fat Girl

watch commercials for these eateries with avidity. I smile at the thin, smiling waitress when she hands diners their menus. I smile as women diners, who, inevitably, are slender and well-kempt, and like the waitress, and like me, are smiling. Male diners often show a bit of *avoir du poids* around the middle, and they smile even bigger than the waitress. I can't believe it when the waitress, now so arduously smiling that the full brace of her white and perfect teeth shows, hauls to the table huge platters circled by gigantic prawns. A tight shot shows diners dipping crustaceans in horseradish–hot cocktail sauce. Then they gaze at each other and smile, smile, smile.

My mouth is dangerous. My lips and my teeth and my tongue and the damp walls of my cheeks are always ready. My mouth wants to bite down on rough bread and hot rare peppered steak and steamed broccoli sprayed with lemon juice. My mouth wants my maternal grandmother's biscuits and sunny-side-up eggs, whose gold yolks rise high above the white circles. My mouth wants potatoes sluiced with gravy and Cobb salad and club sandwiches and ridged potato chips and loathsome onion dip made with sour cream and dry onion soup mix.

When I walk through the kitchen—when I walk through the world—my mouth is on the prowl.

I am frightened of food. I flinch when I consider ice cream, especially flavors beyond strawberry, vanilla, and chocolate. Caramel macadamia crunch might as well be the A-bomb, I am so scared of salty nuts and unctuously sweet caramel. I am scared of the frozen cream that melts along my tongue and walls of my cheeks.

The two couches in my comfortable living room are upholstered with a dark gray fabric. On the skirt of the couch where I most often sit is a stain darker than the upholstery. I never see this stain without thinking of a terrible night.

I could not sleep. I wandered the lightless apartment. Lily the Dachshund, an exceptionally long roan-red dog with an exceptionally long tail, wandered behind me. I opened the freezer and took out a pint of strawberry ice cream and a round-bowled sterling soup spoon and sat on the couch in the moonless dark. Lily the Dachshund, fond of ice cream, nuzzled at my bare feet with her cold black nose.

I sat at the edge of the couch, legs slightly apart. My elbows were on my knees; I was hunched and full of sorrow. I wore a loose cotton nightgown. My breasts hung down inside the gown and swayed. I spooned into my mouth the first chilly strawberry dollop. Cream melted on my tongue, which didn't take long, because the ice cream was soft. I spooned in another bite. I wanted to say to the ice cream, "I love you." I wanted to say, "You are my mother." I wanted to whimper, "Mama, Mama, Mama." I wanted to weep.

I spooned out the last bite for Lily. The ice cream, by then, was runny. As I put the spoon into the empty

Fat Girl

carton so that Lily could lick it, ice cream dribbled down the couch's skirt. That dribble's what stained the couch.

I am scared of the big, hot hole my mouth is. My mouth always wants something and most of what my mouth wants, I can't give it.

two

"A story untold could be the
one that kills you."

—Pat Conroy,
Beach Music

I never do not know what I weigh. Mornings, early, I write in a journal. The second entry I make, after I note date and time, is what I weigh. Were I to forget what I weighed on, say, the day that my older daughter graduated from high school or the day that my first book was accepted for publication, I could look in my journals and find those numbers.

When I come home from my morning walk, I strip. Between what would be my waist if I had one and my pudenda hang fat rolls. The rolls form swags, drapes of loose fat that droop between my hip bones. My freckled breasts lay flat on my chest, and from under my breasts sweat runs.

I step onto the scales. "Dear God," I whisper, "please, please, please." God knows what I want. I want those fat lumps of me gone, gone, gone.

My flesh resists loss. My fat holds on for dear life, holds on under my bratwurst arms and between my clabber thighs, along my moist back and under my fat-lined chest, where my heart thumps with the exertion of hauling twenty, thirty, even forty extra pounds. When I take my week's dirty clothes—sheets, pillowcases, towels, tea towels, the bath mat, my fat-lady underwear and fat-lady blouses and pants with the elastic waistbands—to the laundry, the proprietor weighs the bag. Unless I've entertained, the bag weighs eighteen to twenty pounds. I am two laundry bags too fat.

Two pounds a week, if I'm lucky, is the most I can subtract from myself. I go to bed hungry. I find it easy to understand how famished pioneers roast a red-breasted robin on a green twig over a hastily built fire. I get out of bed and walk around the rooms. I am dizzy. My stomach growls. I look out the window at stars and moon. The moon is far away. The stars are farther.

One-third of the world is hungrier than I am. And they are not on a diet.

I know so many diets. The pineapple and watermelon diet I stayed on for ten days. I did the seven-oranges-per-day diet. I did the rice diet—one cup of rice and one-half cup of fruit three times a day. I did canned diet drinks, four cans a day. I did water-packed tuna and asparagus diets. I do three-day juice fasts. I do these fasts on Friday, Saturday and Sunday because by Saturday noon about all I can do is sprawl on the couch and read novels that have plots strong enough to carry me.

My favorite diet is the hot dog diet. I found this diet taped to the refrigerator in the house where my skinny adulterous lover lived with his wife and children. Toward the last days of my disastrous second marriage I was madly in love with this guy. His wife was a heroic fighter of fat and it was she who had taped the hot dog diet to the refrigerator door. He hated fat on a woman and wasn't shy about saying so. Both she and I loved her skinny husband so much that we were willing to starve ourselves in order to hold his attention. We went hungry and swam up and down the hot and noisy municipal pool so that he would run his long cool bony fingers down the length of our famished bodies.

For women the diet is three hot dogs and three buns per day. For men it's four dogs and four buns. I use all-beef hot dogs. I lay out on the counter a piece of paper towel folded over twice. I am cheered if the paper towel is printed with jolly flowers or cute Dutch boys and girls. I place hot dog and bun on the paper. I stick a fork into the dog to make holes and then I carry the paper towel with dog and a white bread bun to the microwave. In my little oven, dog and bun are ready to go in one minute. The dog should be sweating fat droplets when you take it out. I slather the dog with grainy Dijon mustard and sweet pickle relish and I stand at the counter and stuff into my mouth the hot dog deliciousness. You don't even dirty a dish.

When I put myself onto a weight-loss regime, I am my own strict mistress. I stick to my diet. I eat not a crumb that isn't assigned me. Not one. But for all that I starve and for all that I walk an hour and ride miles to nowhere on the exercise bike, my fat holds on. When I put myself on three- and four-month-long strict diets and feel weak and tired and hungry, I tell myself, "Remember this the next time you slather butter on a piece of thick whole-grain toast. Remember how miserable you were and for how long. Remember going to bed so hungry you could not sleep."

I never remember. When I lose weight and bite into thick porous toast that has soaked up butter so bright in its taste that it surely carries sunshine in its fat globules, I murmur, "How delicious." And I wonder where weight goes when I lose it.

I am a sucker for Before and After. In print ads, melancholy ultra-obese women transform themselves into trim, cheerful blondes. Television commercials, though, are best, because the fatty tells how he lost his hundred pounds through diet and exercise and whatever product the commercial's selling. The now-slender fatty rhapsodizes about changes in his life. He looks out of the television screen into viewers' eyes. "You can do it," he says. "I did." I feel I've known him all my life and that he's known me. I feel that he cares more about what happens to me than does anyone else in the world.

I fantasize rapid weight loss: "Now if I lose one pound per day for thirty days, I can fit into my pale blue dress with the middy collar or button up my blouse that's printed with tiny goldfish." I am enamored of what I call the Swiss Diet Plan, where you are in a clinic in Switzerland that specializes in weight loss. They knock you out for six weeks and feed you vitamins intravenously and turn you over every few hours so you don't get suppurating bedsores. You sleep while you lose.

I like to imagine that I am having liposuction. A masked doctor vacuums fat from my belly and thighs and unspeakably huge butt. A glass vat next to the operating table fills with tubs o' lard, and the doctor, voice muffled by his mask, tells his nurses that he's siphoned forty pounds out of me. They laugh.

Not only do I visualize weight loss and picture myself as doe-eyed and willowy as the late Audrey Hepburn, but I buy clothes for this thin me. I like clothes. I purchase some amazing blouse in a size that wouldn't begin to button and pants that never in my lifetime will zip. The sales associate, which is what salesladies are called these days, inevitably looks puzzled and asks, "Would you like to try those on?" I arrange my features in my most sincere expression and say, "No, I am buying these for my daughter."

I have an entire closet where I hang clothes that

Fat Girl

fit the person I would like to be. Some of these dresses are twenty years old. Some are older. Others, I have squeezed myself into a few times. Some I have never worn; the hang tags dangle off the sleeves.

Dress-up clothes I have in all sizes, from normal to extremely fat. My fat clothes are black. It's easier to convince yourself you look presentable enough to leave the house if you wear a black crepe dress or black trousers and black blousy top. I annul myself in black.

When I am really fat, as opposed to medium or mildly fat, I have trouble pulling on pantyhose, even pantyhose made for fat women. I sit on my bed to put on pantyhose. When I am really fat, I have to lean over my enormous stomach to get at my feet, so as to start pulling the flimsy stockings on. I huff and puff and sweat and get breathless. If I am not careful, I tear the stocking, or, if the pantyhose don't have enough give, then when I stand and pull the waistband up over my thighs and my stomach and buttocks, the pantyhose get long vertical runs and I have to take them off and get out a new package and start again. Sometimes I get the pantyhose pulled up, but I am too big for them and the waistband won't go farther than my crotch. I toss these and get out another pair. By this time sweat has run down from under my arms and from between my breasts. I am angry by this time too, and ashamed, and disgusted for being such a grotesque and grunting hog. I am red in the face, wet with sweat and slightly sick to my stomach.

Judith Moore

You can't hide fat. You can hang about the house until the sun goes down (something I did more often before armed robbers began to stalk our neighborhood). But you can't hide your stomach and your pallid arms. The body will not lie for you. No matter what a fat woman wears, a fat woman looks like a fat fat woman. Lots of happy talk goes on about tricks the Rubenesque gal can do to make herself appear slim. Colorful scarves help, I've read; bright colors and interesting prints draw attention away from your apple face and poked-out gut. Dark colors promise to hide the less-than-ideal figure.

I go on a sunny afternoon to a mall store that sells fat clothes. A sales associate who's young enough to be my daughter carries black skirts and black tee-tops and black jackets that I have selected. She tells me she'll be back to check. Sweat pops out on my forehead. Sweat forms under my breasts and blooms beneath my armpits. I'm freshly bathed and generously sprayed with deodorant and good Guerlain perfume, and yet I start to smell. I smell meaty. I hate these clothes and I hate this store. I have gained weight and nothing dressy fits. My most commodious dress-up skirt grips around the waist so hard that the hook and eyes tear off; the jacket strains at the buttons. By the time I get myself stuffed into this black synthetic fabric fat suit my face is bright red and the sweat has quit popping out on my forehead and now runs down into my eyes, and the salt makes my eyes smart. The skirt comes down to my ankles. But the jacket buttons across my bosom.

Fat Girl

The dressing room curtain slides open. "How are we doing?" the sales associate asks. She must be accustomed to fat women trying on fat clothes and her gaze at me is kind.

I have been taking a hard look at myself in the dressing room's three-way mirror. Who am I kidding? My curly hair forms a corona around my round scarlet face, from the chin of which fat has begun to droop. My swollen feet in their black Mary Janes show from beneath the bottom hem of the ridiculous swaying skirt. The dressing room smells of my beefy stench. I should cry but I don't. I am used to this. I am inured.

My svelte little mother, about whom you will hear more later, was wont to lower her voice and say, about a fat woman, "Poor dear." If she disliked the poor dear more than she liked her, and she usually did, she added, "Sad to see a woman let herself go that way."

I study myself in the department store three-way mirror. I whisper, "Poor dear," and cram myself back into my old clothes and wipe the sweat off my face and gather my new black fat suit over my arm and pay and leave.

What somebody who's never been fat feels sure will happen next is that I waddle straight to the mall ice cream store and console myself with a banana split. I've never eaten a banana split. I like to look at the pictures though. The whipped cream set atop the supine banana swirls upward into peaks and the cherries' jaunty stems rise out of the cherry belly button. I also do not avail myself of the white chocolate chip macadamia nut cookies, which, on occasion, I have chomped with great pleasure. I do not stop in front of the candy store and admire chocolate creams, although when I pass that store I do consider how much I like maple cream coated in chocolate.

What I in fact do is walk, head down, out of the mall. The plastic shopping bag that holds my now tissue-wrapped and folded ugly black fat suit is heavy. I am heavy. I am ashamed and I am resigned to my shame.

The day that fellow told me I was too fat to fuck I wasn't even that fat. I weighed thirty pounds less than I weigh now when, truly, I am ready-for-market fat. Why I am so fat this time (there is always some reason) is that I quit smoking. I haven't smoked one cigarette in three years.

I quit smoking in part because almost everyone I knew quit smoking. I was bothered by the way I had begun to lie about smoking. I didn't come right out and say, "I do not smoke." What I did was I didn't smoke when I was with people who did not smoke. When I went out, I hid my cigarette pack in the bottom of my purse under my eyeglass case. I had no idea that I, my clothes and my hair reeked of smoke.

When I hosted a dinner party or invited a couple for drinks and talk, I walked upstairs to my workroom before my guests rang the doorbell and smoked a cigarette. I smoked the cigarette right down to the filter and stubbed the filter out in the ashtray. Then I sprayed my workroom with Guerlain's Jicky, the same scent that Jackie Kennedy often wore, and I hid the ashtray. I rushed, then, down the stairs to the bathroom and scrubbed my hands with scented soap. I brushed my teeth and swished blue mouthwash over my teeth and tongue and the interior walls of my cheeks. The mouthwash stung.

Dinner with friends always was fun. Talk was spirited and the food usually good. I am a fat woman who's comfortable eating in the company of thin people, and, come to think of it, all my friends are slender. I forked up salad and poached salmon decorated with tissuethin cucumber slices, or if it were winter a ham loaf made with ground smoked ham and veal. I added my two cents to conversation. I slurped wine. Typically, dessert was a chocolate pound cake or a highly praised blueberry bread pudding, or amazing fruit shortcakes I concocted with rich shortbread cookies and red raspberries, gold raspberries or sliced ripe peaches dredged in sugar, topped by cream whipped close to butter.

I would put water on for coffee and assemble the pound cake and ice cream or the shortcake. That's when I would long for a cigarette. No way could I escape and light up. I became restless and irritable. My guests seemed increasingly less vivid. A man of whom I am fond talked about his mother and her lonely death. I fixed a look onto my face that I hoped said sympathy and wondered if I dared go into the bathroom and light up.

Here by myself, smoking while I ate never occurred to me. That I could not smoke made me want to puff,

puff, puff. I wanted that white, fresh, unlit cigarette between my fingers. I wanted the match flare and the sulfur smell from the match head. I wanted to fill myself with smoke. I wanted everyone to disappear, to evanesce, to float away out those windows where an hour earlier that falling sun had gilded the glass. No one needed to say good-bye, no one needed to press my hand and thank me for a lovely meal, a lovely evening, a lovely time. No, no, no. Just go. I will throw your jackets, your purses, out the windows, down where you parked your cars. Just go. Go now. Leave me alone to shake that cigarette from the pack and light it up.

Sometimes I broke down and apologized, acted (and felt, and was) contrite and asked if I might smoke. Always everyone said yes, of course, it is your own house, why not?

Finally, the urge to smoke got so bad that when I was with people it was all I thought about. One morning I got up and wrote in my journal that I was sick of smoking. That morning I quit. I haven't smoked another cigarette since.

Over the next eighteen months I gained forty-five pounds. A friend from the East Coast visited. We had not seen one another in that time. When I greeted him at the door his eyes widened at the sight of me. He loves me and I felt sorry for him when he took me to dinner. He is handsome and trim and I knew that people who looked at us must wonder what someone as elegant as he was doing with a bloated old toad like me.

When I'm in a good mood, I have to remind myself

that I am not twenty-five and slim (and I was slim at twenty-five). I not long ago invited over a brilliant man for dinner. We'll call him "George." I like to give that name to everyone to whom I don't want to attach an actual name. George is ten years younger than I am. He's divorced. He's something of a gallant. At the time I invited him, he was not involved with anyone. I have no romantic interest in him, nor would it ever occur to me that anyone as Lincolnesque in height, of average good looks, who's ten years my junior would have any romantic interest in me. I invited him over because I was feeling lonesome and he was someone with whom I liked to talk. I invited him over because my impression always has been that he likes to talk with me.

I tried on three or four outfits before I stuffed myself into black linen pants and a white tissue linen middy shirt. I checked my manicure, to make sure there wasn't the tiniest chip in my polish. I slicked on lipstick. I looked at myself in the mirror. I smiled.

I thought, "Being fat is not the end of the world."

three

"I wanted to be able to bear this.
I have tried to."

—Ovid, *Metamorphoses*, Book X

George arrived his usual twenty minutes late. We kissed. We had not seen each other in several months and he did not gasp at my weight gain. We sat in the living room and sipped at a dry French white wine. We gossiped about mutual friends. George told me how his work at the university was going, which was better than expected, and how his daughter was doing in the expensive college she attended, a college whose tuition was keeping George broke. I fed him a tasty dinner— ahi tuna filet encrusted with toasted black and white sesame seeds, pineapple rice and a teriyaki vegetable stir-fry. Dessert was a small apricot tart purchased from the patisserie run by French pastry cooks with beards so dark that five o'clock shadow darkens their cheeks by noon. George likes to eat and he never gains weight. He cleaned his plate amidst much yum-yum-yum and he finished off the tart.

We repaired to the living room and drank the rest of that dry white wine. Perhaps the principal reason George and I have continued to see one another over many years is our interest in poetry. We both recently had read what the critic Frank Kermode had written about Wallace Stevens and Stevens's fondness for Holderlin. We gushed a bit about Kermode and then George quoted from Archibald MacLeish's poem, "Reasons for Music":

> Why do we labor at the poem
> Age after Age—even an age like
> This one, when the living rock
> No longer lives and the cut stone perishes?—
>
> Holderlin's question. Why be poet
> Now when the meanings do not mean?—
> When the stone shape is shaped stone?—

I felt buoyant. I felt giddy. I felt I could dance. I felt, God help me, as if I were starring in a musical comedy. I plopped down right next to George, unaware right then of how, seating my obese self, I must have shaken the sofa and unaware too that I had pressed my fat black linen-covered thigh against his khaki-covered thigh and my shoulder against his shoulder. What we said, I can't retrieve. I can only tell you that it was the talk of people who are genuinely interested in poetry and that I was having fun and I think George was having fun too.

I was unaware, though, at that moment, of how my excited corpulent flesh gave off so much heat. I must have been like a woodstove, stoked with dry wood. I was unaware that in this excitement my voice rose a half octave and that I spoke faster than I normally would. I was a little drunk, yes, and I'd gone ardent over the poem. After we had arrived at the poem's final lines and read them together—

> Generations of the dying
> Fix the sea's dissolving salts
> In stone, still trees, their branches immovable,
> Meaning
>   the movement of the sea.

—I planted a loud, explosive and exuberant kiss on George's cheek and, as if I were a giddy hundred-pound teenager, squealed, "Oooh, I love you!!"

George jumped. His eyes widened. I broke out in a sweat so heavy that my wet heat must have raised the humidity in the area around the couch. This bloom of perspiration broke the spell for me. George looked shell-shocked. He wriggled toward the end of the couch. I stood up and asked if he'd like coffee and he said he would.

Fat Girl

Perhaps George thought nothing of my leaning in close to him, my pressure against his thigh, his side, his shoulder, my noisy kiss, accompanied by shrill giggles. Perhaps he thought that I'd had too much wine. I had. I hope that's what he thought. I would hate to think that he went away believing that I wanted more than what was between us. What there is, is plenty. (We still see each other. The other night, we read Robert Lowell and nattered about Lowell and Elizabeth Bishop and read "Skunk Hour" and talked about how Lowell beat his first wife, Jean Stafford, poor dear.)

Because I'm overweight and no longer young I feel that I must be careful not to frighten men, or, for that matter, younger women, who might think I take a Sapphic interest in them. I must not hug until I am hugged, kiss unless I am kissed. I tell myself to remember not to be coy, not to cast myself as what would appear a rotund, elderly Shirley Temple. No rolling of the eyes, no noisy glee, no adorable drawl.

So here I am, a self-made fat girl, hidden beneath her self-made padding. The fat pads me like those heavy wrappers movers put around pianos when they move the pianos from house to house. I am protected in fat, protected by fat. In spite of myself, I crawl deeper and deeper into the cave of fat. I add fat, pound by pound by pound.

But the peculiar thing is that I have not eaten that much more than I ate when I was not as fat. When I quit smoking I felt myself slow down. Tobacco speeds you up. Once I didn't have cigarettes, I walked more slowly. I slept longer.

Fat, you are lost inside yourself. You are lost inside your body. The body is the last redoubt. I peer out of my yellow fatty acids into the world. I never can quite get out of my body, not even when I am not fat. When I am thin, I cry easily. I feel too small. I feel weak and woozy. You might say "Aha" and think that a psychological insight has been given you and me. It hasn't. I am afraid that the primary reason that I feel woozy and slight when I am slender is that to keep down my weight I cannot eat enough. I am always hungry.

My doctor does not believe me when I tell him I do not stuff myself, does not believe that I am not the owner of a two-pound box of chocolate-covered cherries. I hate going to him. Since I have packed on the nonsmoking pounds, I have especially hated medical shenanigans. I hate having my breasts smashed down for the mammogram. I hate the weigh-in.

My doctor is tall and rail thin. When I go for my Pap smear, I don't see how Dr. Skinny can stand to touch me, much less to peer between my legs so as to poke and scrape at my worn-out womb. One day I ask how he bears up under these exams and he says, in a tone one can only describe as embittered, "You get used to it."

On a recent Saturday morning I walked to a small shopping district. I love to walk. The street on whose sidewalk I hurried along is two lanes. I was headed north. The sun shone and people, some in pairs and some like me, alone, walked south. I saw no one I knew. I no doubt was walking fast. I tend to walk fast, to hurry along. I do not know what I was thinking. I was wearing black: black pants and black shirt and black jacket, black shoes. Sunglasses. I crouch inside black and screen myself behind dark glasses. I do not want to be seen.

I was fat on this Saturday. I know how fat. I would let a torturer use pliers to pull teeth from the tender gums in the back of my head before I could say what I weigh when I'm fat. What I weigh seems like the secret that must be hid most carefully. That I can hide my fat is an absurd notion. That if I don't tell you what I weigh I will seem less fat, that's absurd too.

What happened that Saturday was that a white Chrysler convertible, top down, sped south, toward me. Four boys were in the convertible, college boys is what they looked like, and probably were. A grin spread across the face of the boy in the front passenger seat and I knew something was coming. "Oink, oink, oink," he squealed. His companions joined him, "Oink, oink, oink." And, a two-fingered high-pitched whistle and "Sooey, sooey, pig." Then they were gone in the stream of traffic and I looked straight ahead from behind my sunglasses and just kept walking. This was not the first time in my life that someone had called out to me, "Sooey, sooey, pig." I was used to being called names, and in a way, I had—and have—ceased to care that people did and do this.

I know that people talk about how since I quit

smoking I gained so much weight. I know they do. They take for granted I gulp down soft drinks and wear out my arm dipping ridged potato chips into sour cream and onion dip. They feel sure that I don't walk farther than from couch to refrigerator. They are wrong.

But no one says out loud one word about how fat you are (unless they're drunk on cans of Budweiser and telling you how you are too fat to fuck). The fat woman is the elephant in the room, the subject about whom no one talks and everyone entertains at least one thought. Friends will not say you've put on a few pounds. But you know it has been on people's minds because when you lose weight the same friends who have been silent about your blimpiness say, "Oh, you look terrific." "Good for you."

Psychology tries to make graphs from lives like mine. Psychology tries to turn unseen moments into measurable events. Psychology needs to locate reasons. Psychology wants to go back to the beginning and ferret out the first act. Psychology must reduce pain, must press it down the way you press down a duck to make pressed duck, the way you reduce a stock; psychology must get pain down onto the page in black and white Psychology, to stay in business, to believe in itself, promises to heal.

Humans are more complex than what psychology can make of us. It is one thing for me to tell you that my mother didn't have enough love to give me or that my father, for years, fled from my life, and that for many years, no matter what Mama did and no matter what I did, I got fatter and fatter. It would be another to get across to you in all its minutia how unhappy I was, how unhappy sometimes I still am. I can't tell you precisely why I was unhappy and neither can psychology.

I have little insight into why I gain and lose and gain and lose. If I hadn't lost so many pounds I would weigh, this morning, at least one thousand pounds. My head would appear tiny atop my giant body. I would feed myself with a shovel. I would have ten stomach rolls and breasts big as punching bags in boxing gyms. How would my size seven-B feet support me? Where would a thousand-pound person eat dinner? And sleep? And go to the bathroom? You would have to hire a winch to lift me from my bed.

Sometimes I think that I should stop bothering with the lose part of gain and lose. I could eschew diets and grow myself larger. Why I don't do this is partly vanity and partly that when I get what I call "really fat" I heave for breath when I walk up stairs and sweat pours off me when I so much as dust the bookshelf or lift Lily the Dachshund, who also is too fat.

People on the street stop me sometimes and ask if Lily is pregnant. I am glad she does not understand them. She slowly wags her long ratlike brown tail. She is not one of those squeaking and squealing miniature Dachshunds who jumps up on your leg and rips your stocking; she's a lengthy standard, and like most standard Dachshunds she's stubborn, even mulish; she is moody and melancholic and quiet.

Lily, however, is always ready to eat. When a slender woman carrying a grease-besotted sack of Kentucky Fried Chicken passes us on the sidewalk near my apartment one afternoon, long Lily rushes forward and grabs a corner of the bag and rips. This happens before I can pull back on Lily's leash and stop her.

The woman screams. I scream. Passersby slow and stare and rush away. A great ruckus ensues—the woman, Lily, me, the Colonel's chicken. The sack has spilled out on the sidewalk. Lily has grabbed a drumstick. I wrest the chicken from between her sharp teeth. Lily snarls. Lily resists. Meat pulls off the bone as I pull the drumstick from Lily's mouth. My hand is sticky with dog drool and chicken grease. Crunchers from the chicken skin have gotten stuck under my perfectly polished fingernails.

The young woman, an exceptionally pretty blonde, is red-faced. She says my dog has ruined her dinner. She asks, wasn't I paying any attention when my dog grabbed her food? I apologize. The woman says her entire dinner is destroyed. Lily, whom I have short-leashed, is now trying to get the chicken breast. There is also a container of cole slaw and a roll and napkins and a plastic fork on the filthy sidewalk.

I have money in my pocket. I take out a twenty and hand it to the woman, who, when I look closely, I see is more girl than woman, and who can't weigh 110 pounds. "Thank you," she says and gives me a dirty look and walks off fast.

I kick the chicken into the gutter. I hold tight to Lily's leash with one hand and with the other pick up

Fat Girl

the torn sack, the cole slaw, the fork, the drumstick. I consider saving the cole slaw for later. I think that this chicken dinner didn't cost more than $5.99, and now because I was ashamed and embarrassed and because I am fat and I have allowed my poor Dachshund to become fat, I have handed over to this blonde bitch my hard-earned twenty buckaroos. Fuck her.

You would think that during the three decades, off and on, when I blathered away in one therapy after another that I would have talked about fatness and how I starved myself and how I sometimes used up three hours of a perfectly good morning running circles on a track and doing ridiculous jumping jacks and hopping and clapping to Richard Simmons's *Sweatin' to the Oldies* videotape. You would think that I might have confessed that while I did this running and jumping and hopping I saw myself as thin and strong and fit; I saw a golden girl. But I didn't mumble one word about my fatness or my longings to be lovely to even one therapist. I was too ashamed. Nor did any therapist to whom I went ever inquire about why I was fat.

How many mornings I've bounced through Richard Simmons's *Sweatin' to the Oldies "2,"* I don't know. The only room in my apartment whose floor is not over another apartment is the kitchen. Because I do not wish to disturb my kindly downstairs neighbor, I place the portable television-VCR atop the kitchen table and pop in the tape. *Sweatin' to the Oldies* is set in Pop's Diner, a neon-lit fifties-era soundstage. Spotlights sweep across sixteen exercisers, men and women, lined up behind Simmons. "Let's sweat! Let's get those hands going!" Simmons yowls. He leads us through a warm-up. "The Locomotion" plays in the background. Simmons and his sixteen sing along—"Everybody's doin' a brand new dance now. (Come on, baby, do the loco-motion.)" Simmons lifts his tanned arms and mimics pulling the bell on an old-fashioned locomotive. He wears a sleeveless jersey and spandex shorts. It appears that he shaves beneath his arms. His curly brown hair encircles his head and he opens his eyes wide and he smiles and smiles and smiles.

I know some of Simmons's story. He grew up in New Orleans. He sold pralines on the streets to get extra money. One night on *Larry King Live* I heard Simmons say, "To me, food was love. I couldn't wait to open the refrigerator." When he was eight, little Richard weighed two hundred pounds. As a teenager he weighed three hundred pounds. When he was sixteen he decided to thin down for good, and apparently did, although he told Larry King that he lost lots of the weight by vomiting food. Eventually, he went out to Los Angeles and eventually, after working for a while as a waiter, he opened an exercise studio for fat people. When he was fifty he wrote his autobiography—*Still Hungry—After All These Years*—which I have never read.

I also know that many of the sixteen people following along with Simmons's mimed bell pulling and leg lifting were once much fatter than they are now. Maybe half the men and women now are fairly slender; the rest range from heavyset to obese. I've sweated and struggled through this tape for so long that these

Fat Girl

Simmons exercisers are old friends. Morning after morning, of course, these people never change. The two-hundred-pound woman in the black tights and purple top never stops smiling. The butch-looking gal in spandex shorts and a tee never stops executing her gestures aggressively.

I never know quite how I will make myself dance through the sixty-some minutes that the tape lasts. One way I keep hopping and sliding and deep-knee-bending is to focus on one of the exercisers. I know most of their names. Why I know their names is that at the end of *Sweatin' to the Oldies* the participants, under flashing neon, vogue down a runway. While they prance and shimmy, their names and the number of pounds they've lost flash on the screen beneath them. Celia Powell, who is still quite a big girl, is 110 pounds lighter. Michele Matz, who has some pounds to go, lost 20. Nancy Nineger, another large girl, dieted and exercised away 35 pounds. Tobie Salcido, also still hefty, lost 135. Slender Laverne Jones lost 65 pounds. Chubby Lisa Blackburn in her pink shirt and pink tights freed herself of 110 pounds. One of my favorite exercisers, Tami Williams, who wears a roomy purple shirt and black tights and a persistent smile, has lost 155 pounds. Slender and lithe Elijah Jones, handsome in an orange shirt, has dropped 285 pounds. Michael Hebranko, who wears a pale blue shirt and black pants, took from himself 740 pounds. The adorable, butch Aaron McCallister, whose movements are so forceful, has lost 134 pounds. I hope Aaron is happy.

Judith Moore

I also hope Michael Hebranko is okay. I read that
after he performed on *Sweatin' to the Oldies* early in the
1990s that he began to gain back his weight. In 1999
he got up to 1,100 pounds. He went into a hospital
weight-loss program and got down to 650. That was in
2001, when he was fifty years old. I don't know what's
happened to him and I'm afraid to ask.

I do the loco-motion, I pull that train bell. I make
myself smile. I sing along with "Big Girls Don't Cry,"
"Respect," "Breakin' Up Is Hard to Do," and "Pretty
Woman." I sing with Tami Williams, who wears the ca-
pacious purple top and black tights, who is so brave to
have taken off 155 pounds. These are my brothers and
my sisters; they are my family. They eat too much and
they get too fat. Their presence on streets is a specta-
cle. Their bodies provoke disgust, even from people who
call themselves friends.

I love the men and women on this tape. I love their
faces and I admire their exuberance and courage.

four

"Deep is the well of the past."

—Thomas Mann,
Joseph and His Brothers

Sometimes my whole life seems to be stories about fat.

Every year on the Sunday nearest the Feast of St. Francis of Assisi our Episcopal parish here in Berkeley holds a blessing of the animals. I love to get Lily the Dachshund bathed and brushed to a sheen for this service. I love to sit on a hard wooden pew in the sunlit sanctuary with Lily stretched across my lap. I love the way that Lily, excited, takes on a doggy odor. I love the moment when the priest arrives at my pew and dribbles holy water on Lily's roan-red head.

I had been on a diet through spring and summer

before a recent animal blessing. So when I got dressed that morning, I went all-out. I wore my black hat made by hand by an honest-to-God milliner and I wore sheer pantyhose and black two-inch heels and a black linen A-line dress with sleeves that hit above the elbow. I didn't think I looked like a movie star but I thought I looked pretty.

After the service we stood in the parish courtyard. The day was warm and the sky clear. Perhaps two hundred of us chatted while dogs sniffed other dogs and cats and birds peered from cages. A teenage boy had a snake wound around his neck and there were hamsters and lop-ear rabbits and even a goldfish bowl in which three fish swam in the bowl's turbulent waters. The parish photographers snapped photos.

I was happy. I'd lost forty pounds. I fit into my dress. I liked my hat and I liked wearing a hat. I smiled and even preened a bit as the photographers shot photos.

The next Sunday, I attended the eight o'clock service, held in a small chapel in the church's undercroft. Before I headed into the chapel, which always smelled of beeswax candles, I stood at the bulletin board outside the sanctuary and studied blessing of the animals photographs. I saw me with Lily, and my knees—literally—went weak.

My happy smile had made my mouth crooked; my eyes were slightly unfocused and I appeared frantic and theatrically crazy, as if I were the heroine in a silent film desperate to escape a mustachioed villain. My black hat, out from whose brim my curls poked, looked bizarre. The hat was a bad idea. The bare arms were a bad idea too. The worst was that the black linen dress pulled across my hips and the way my stomach bulged out I might have been six months pregnant.

Ten minutes into mass, when the lay reader stepped up to read from the Old Testament lesson, I was gulping and swallowing air. I was having a panic attack. I frequently have panic attacks, so I knew just what to do and I did it. I counted backward from one hundred. I breathed slowly. I reminded myself that I was not going to throw up, I was not going to shout "fuck" and scare the hell out of the dozen other communicants. I grabbed my purse and fled out the door and snatched that photo off the bulletin board and walked home fast as I could.

Upstairs in my workroom I turned on the paper shredder and fed in the photograph. I watched the photo turn to confetti. I thought about nights I went to bed hungry so as to fit into that black linen dress (which hangs now in the closet, unworn for several years). I don't know what I did the rest of that Sunday. I do know that I did not go back to church for weeks and that when church people asked me why, I lied and said I had been really, really busy.

It may come as a surprise to you—or maybe it won't—but I often do not realize that I am fat, or how fat I am. When I am by myself I don't tend to think about how I appear. I think about what I am doing. So when I see photographs like that taken at the pet blessing, I am shocked by the difference between how I believed I

Judith Moore

looked and how I did look. This has happened before; I have believed I looked acceptably attractive, or even pretty, and then saw photographs that showed my wide butt and bulging stomach and those arms as big as big bolognas that hang from deli ceilings.

Plus, as I age, I don't even want to look at my face. From my father I inherited droopy upper eyelids that, as I get older, droop more. My father could have been mistaken for Charles Laughton or Whittaker Chambers or Harold Bloom. He had the same outsized morose face as those guys and he had the heavy stomach that hung, in rolls, from his breasts.

He was six-four and at his fattest he must have weighed three hundred pounds. He was enormous waddling fat, and fat and huge daily sadness probably killed him. He was seventy-three when he dropped dead. He had just finished putting up pints of apple butter in his kitchen in rural Illinois. He made extraordinary apple butter. (I have his recipe—the only spice he used is cinnamon, and why the apple butter never scorches is that he baked it in the oven at 300 degrees until the fruit thickened.)

Three times in his life he was thin: from birth until he turned six and his mother died; in college and law school until he married my mother; and for a year or so after my mother tossed him out. My mother, when I would ask her about the divorce, never forgot to point out that one reason she threw my father out was because he was so fat. She grabbed my chin in her hand

43

Fat Girl

and squeezed tight. The spit gathered up into a lake in my mouth. She looked down into my eyes. "Listen," she said, her breath hot on my face, "he crushed me. Buried me alive."

My mother wasn't fat, although in her forties she tended to run to wide hips and doubled chin. One spring when we lived in northern Florida, she drank Metrecal for breakfast and lunch; by summer she was twirling before her full-length mirror and singing, "Look who just starved ten ugly years off herself!"

Brown-skinned Mary, called "Black Mary" to distinguish her from my father's grandmother's sister, whose name was also Mary, took care of my father when he was a child and later took care of me. I visited Mary when she was old and blind and skinny. She hadn't been skinny always. When I was a toddler her stomach was fat and soft as pillows. Her face was fat. The day I visited, she rocked in a high-back chair and talked. She told me about my father when he was little and my father's mother and my father's grandparents. She gave me recipes that had been my father's favorites and I wrote them down. Her recipe for butterscotch meringue pie is tucked in my Fannie Farmer.

My father told me how, after his mother died, the casket that held her body sat in the living room. Before they closed the coffin, my father's father lifted my father, six years old then, up in his arms. He dangled him over his mother. He said, "Kiss Mama good-bye." My father was afraid he'd fall from his father's slack grip, down onto his dead mother. He kissed her mouth. He said it was all he could do to keep from throwing up on the body.

Once the funeral was over my father—Hamilton Jr., "Ham" for short—moved across the street to his maternal grandparents' house. His grandmother, after her only daughter's death, took to her bed and refused to eat. Already a sparrow of a woman, she grew so frail she had to be helped to what she called "the commode." She told my father that her daughter's death was his father's fault, which it well may have been. No one told my father why his mother's death might have been his father's fault, but my father nevertheless came to hate his father—Big Ham—and he never forgave him his mother's demise.

Big Ham couldn't have been more than five and a half feet tall. Maybe he weighed 180. His cowboy boots added height and he topped his round head with a high-crowned Stetson that added more. By the time I knew him he was in his sixties. He had floppy double chins and his belly was one of those hard pots that strains trousers. He had some Indian in him that showed in his cheekbones. He was maybe the finest quail and pheasant hunter anybody knew and was sharp with money, in buying and selling land, and at the poker table. There was talk, my father told me, that the death of his mother hardly stopped Big Ham from the work of making money and the play of chasing whores. "Peroxide blondes," my father said, were his father's favorites.

My father took sick after they buried his mother. He ran fevers. He awoke from nightmares, screaming for his mother, and he fought sleep because he feared the bad dreams. They carried a canvas cot into his room. Black Mary slept there.

Like his maternal grandmother, my father couldn't eat. At noon, my father's grandfather came home from his bank for dinner (he owned the bank). Ham sat at the table, with his grandfather. He pushed food around his plate. He said, "I'm not hungry."

Mary made egg custard for her little invalid. She spooned the custard into my father's mouth. My father told me that he could still hear Mary say, "Your mama would want you to eat." Mary made my father's favorites— waffles, chicken drumsticks dipped in egg-and-flour batter and deep-fried in lard, Monte Cristo sandwiches (thinly sliced chicken breast, ham, Swiss cheese on white bread with the crust cut away, then dipped in beaten egg and fried, like French toast, in butter), potato salad with piccalilli stirred in, tiny new green peas from the garden, lemon meringue pie, fudge cake, banana pudding. When he balked, Mary didn't let up. "Eat for your mama."

Big Ham married again, within a year of his first wife's death. He married my father's first-grade teacher. In a holiday mood, Big Ham fetched my father home from his grandparents' house. His father put an arm around her and announced, "This is your new mother."

My father waited until his father and the new wife began to yowl and giggle in the back bedroom and then, wearing pajamas and his robe that was printed with brown buffalo and Indians and teepees, he ran across the street to his grandparents' house. If there were words between his father and grandparents about the nighttime escape, my father did not remember them. He never lived in his father's house again.

My father said that around about third grade he began to take on height, and that he was always hungry. Grandfather every month marked a line on the basement wall that showed how tall Ham was. Some months, he grew one-half inch. By fourth grade, he was Grandfather's height—five feet six inches. Grandfather weighed 135 pounds; my father weighed 180.

Nothing fit. Grandmother bought grown men's clothes that she and Mary altered to fit. "Fatso, Fatso," boys yelled at school. And of course they played with the name Ham—he was "Porker" and "Baked Ham" and "Hamlet." He told himself he did not care. He made one hundreds on his papers and A+'s on his report cards. He was put forward one grade. He lived in the hugest house in town. His father held title to land in half the county. His grandfather owned the bank.

Here is where Kathleen, the girl who will be my mother, shows up. About three years after my father's mother was buried, the fall of 1924 if my arithmetic is correct (and it may be off a year or even two years), my mother's mother—Grammy, I eventually would call her—drove up in a taxi and got out at the home of her twenty-five-year-old son, Carl. This son was the only child from her first marriage. With her in the taxi was eight-year-old Kathleen, by husband number two, whose name I never knew.

Fat Girl

It was the middle of the night. Kathleen was weary. She and her mother had been on the train for two days, riding coach from Indiana to Oklahoma. The eight-year-old who in twenty years will suffer the torments of the damned to become my mother had a heart-shaped face under strawberry-blonde hair cut in a Dutch-boy bob. She lugged onto the porch one piece of luggage and her rag doll.

The son, Carl, unmarried, had begun his first job, teaching organ and music theory at Oklahoma A&M College. His mother was forty-two, perhaps forty-four, even forty-five. She shaved her age. She had shucked Kathleen's father, a Folgers coffee salesman, in Indianapolis, Indiana, and was on her way to Los Angeles, following after her newest man. (When I was a toddler, I often heard her sing one of her favorite songs—"My man, I love him so, I'll never let him go.") The Roaring Twenties were roaring. Calvin Coolidge had been elected by a huge majority. Money was begetting money. The mother and her new "beau" planned to open a popcorn stand at the La Brea tar pits in Los Angeles, and then go on to the Klondike in Alaska, where they intended to pan for gold.

The fat boy will become my father and the blue-eyed girl deserted by her mother will become my mother. Deserted *is* the correct word. Through the girl's ten years of schooling, the mother returned only occasionally and never stayed long and never took the daughter with her. She came back to Carl and Kathleen only when she needed money or when a heartbreak was fresh. As for the girl's father, no one mentioned him. No one mentioned Carl's father, either.

Carl, who one day will be my uncle and who will be incredibly kind to me, was, then, a wide-eyed handsome romantic fellow and was not and never would be fat. Lucky him! With his half sister ensconced in his home he could no longer bring home the bright-cheeked country boys who'd come to A&M to buff their Chopin Nocturnes to a dreamy polish. He could no longer swank about in his watered silk smoking jacket and pluck out "I Wish I Could Shimmy Like My Sister Kate" on his ukulele and serve such violent cocktails—Pink Ladies and Singapore Slings—that these farm- and country-town-reared lads, paralyzed by flattery and Prohibition alcohol, tossed about in bed with him, rattling coiled bedsprings and making goose feathers fly out the striped pillow ticks. He renounced his roosterish ways and cooked his little sister's meals, washed and ironed and mended clothing. He brushed and trimmed her Dutch-boy bob, scrubbed behind her ears, snipped her toe- and fingernails. He supported her on his modest salary.

Carl's and my father's grandparents' houses stood two blocks apart. Carl's was the brown cottage off an alley, and my father's grandparents' a mansion two stories high with balconies and screened porches, set on an entire block to itself, with white lattice pergola, a fountain from which a stone dolphin arcs, an ice house

Fat Girl

and a servants' cottage that offered more square feet than Carl and Kathleen's entire house. My father, on his way to and from school and town, passed Carl's house.

The first time my father noticed her, the girl who would become my mother was in Carl's side yard, hanging upside down by her knees from a tree limb. Her skirt fell over her head, exposing white underpants and a flat ivory belly darkened by a pool of belly button.

My father was in his sixties when he told me this. His eyes were closed and he smiled.

five

"Hooks that tear through flesh
Even as they bind it."

—Robert Polito,
"Evidence," *Doubles*

My father talked often about Mary's kitchen. The aromas that issued from that kitchen overruled all other smells at his grandparents' house. Even upstairs with his door closed, my father knew if it was baked chicken and corn bread stuffing or pork loin and fried apples or chuck roast and potatoes or Mary's devil's food layer cake trimmed in dark fudge frosting. Years later, when my father was in his hospital bed after heart surgery and needed to dissuade morphine-induced nightmare visions from return, he roamed his memory of Mary's chicken and dumplings, Mary's butter beans simmered

Fat Girl

with pork hock, Mary's chicken pot pie, Mary's apricot upside-down cake, Mary's chess pie.

My father sat at the kitchen table while Mary eviscerated stewing hens and molded meatballs and whipped meringue. If she was cutting corn off the cob for corn and green bean succotash, he took the knife and cut corn for her. If she was straining the Concord grape pulp for grape jelly, he held the cheesecloth down tight across the jelly pan. If she and Grandmother were making the white fruitcakes Grandmother gave at Christmas, he cracked walnuts and chopped citron and the candied red cherries.

When his grandparents and Mary were asleep, my father tiptoed down the stairs to the kitchen to raid the refrigerator. He said that he always knew what was in the then relatively new GE refrigerator, one of the first, my father said, in town. The presence in the refrigerator of certain dishes—cold roast beef or ham, pies of all kinds, green seedless grapes and Bing cherries—was particularly compelling. He opened the refrigerator's door and pulled out wax-paper-draped platters. The refrigerator's hermetically sealed compressor thumped while my father finished off roasts and gelatin salads. He spooned cold gravy into his mouth and let the gravy melt across his tongue until his warm mouth induced meaty flavors to bloom. He carved away thin slices of ham and dangled the pink slices above his open mouth. He cut one after another slivers of pie, after each sliver saying, "This will be the last. I'll eat no more."

Judith Moore

"Why do you think you ate so much?" I asked him, once.

"I was hungry," he said. But my father, who acquired an LLD from the University of Chicago and who wrote textbooks for the American Bar Association, was not ignorant, and he was not incapable of self-examination. He added, his baggy face anguished, that he was sure that his hunger was connected to his mother's death, and the gloom that descended over his grandparents after she died. Food, he said, filled the gap left by her death. Food comforted him. "But that," he added, "is an overgeneralization."

In 1928, my father was fourteen, an inch short of six feet, and weighed two-hundred-plus pounds. He sweat through clothes even in winter and the elastic on his socks and his shorts cut into his flesh and left red marks. When he caught sight of himself in downtown plate-glass windows he could not believe this was who he was. His belly rode before him and his buttocks stood high, like Africans', and his buttocks ground, up and down, giant turbines propelling his flesh. He wore his trousers pulled up to mid-belly; the trousers pulled against his fat.

Naked, before he stepped into the shower, he saw that his stomach hung down over his penis and his breasts were pendulous as women's. His pale skin had stretched to accommodate his fat and the stretching left scars. The scars looked like lightning bolts. He barely could bend over to tie his shoes. And his feet were so

53

wide—quadruple D's—that he had to be driven to the nearest city for shoes.

Grandmother and Grandfather, if you put them on the scale together, didn't weigh much more than my father alone. Seated, at the table, with them, or in easy chairs in the library, or passing them in hallways, my father feared he'd injure his trim and tiny grandparents if he so much as touched them. Grandmother, whom my father loved so much that he tended to bow his head when he spoke of her, forbade mention of my father's astonishing corpulence. "A phase," she said, "a spurt of growth." She never used the word "fat." She preferred "stocky" and "big-boned" and "on the heavy side."

Of course, my father wanted to be thin. He shunned desserts. He eschewed Mary's hot breads. He avoided breakfast. He starved until he had vicious headaches that aspirin would not quell. He stayed on these self-imposed diets for three days or a week and then he gave them up and tiptoed downstairs to the thrumming refrigerator and spooned leftovers into the great emptiness that was his stomach. "And perhaps the emptiness that was my heart," he said, thirty years ago when he was still alive and weighed at least three hundred pounds.

But his grandparents, he assured me, loved him, and treated him well. And he loved them, and loved Mary, who he felt devoted her life to him after his mother's death. "I was not a happy child, though," he said.

He couldn't play sports—couldn't, of course, run, and couldn't throw or catch or climb ropes or dive. His grandmother got him excused from intramural games and from gymnasium and swimming. Boys Ham's age generally didn't like him but girls even older than he was wanted him for a friend. These girls asked his advice on how to get boys to fall in love with them. These girls summoned him to their houses on Saturday and Sunday afternoons. They made fudge and buttery popcorn that left a glow on his fingertips. They tried on dresses and asked his opinion. When boys deserted them and they were dateless, they invited him as their escort to movies and dances. Grandmother taught him to waltz. Except for breaking out in sweat that ran in sheets inside his stiff shirts and his woolen suits, he loved dancing, loved showing off the girl with dips and turns, loved the new songs he heard on the radio, played by college-boy bands for high school dances— "Blue Skies," "East of the Moon, West of the Stars," "My Heart Stood Still."

That same year, 1928, Kathleen was twelve years old, two years younger than Ham. She did not want people to know that she and Carl did not share the same father; she used her brother's last name. Although it was not true, they both said that their father was dead. Carl's father regularly wrote to Carl and sent him five- and ten-dollar bills on his birthday and at Christmas. Where was Kathleen's father? Nobody was saying. Was she born out of wedlock? Nobody knew. He never visited. No letters from him arrived in the mailbox affixed to Carl's cottage. All Kathleen knew is what her mother said: "He didn't want me to have you." It's not as if Carl and Kathleen's mother wrote that often either. Mostly, she sent jokey postcards printed with cartoons or picture postcards from California, Alaska, Montana, Wyoming, Idaho, and once from Walla Walla, Washington, where, she wrote, her "beau" must spend some time. Forty years later my mother realized that Walla Walla was the location of the state prison.

Kathleen entered high school in 1930. Carl allowed her to wear high-heeled pumps, lipstick and rouge. She ran with sons and daughters of town merchants and college professors. She won elections to student council and was pledged by a prominent high school sorority. She took voice lessons. She sang the national anthem with the drum and bugle corps for Friday auditorium. She starred in operettas. She had a crush on a tall boy called Skipper. They went out a few times, but when Kathleen wouldn't spread her lovely legs for him Skipper dropped her.

My father swore that from the first time he saw my mother—hanging upside down from that tree—he had an eye for her. His last year of high school, before he went away to Missouri to college, they dated. My mother refused to go steady with my father, and when other boys asked her out, she accepted. Mostly, my father visited her and helped her clean house and iron Carl's shirts and chop onions and stew meat for dinner. She played the piano and sang "Blue Skies" and "Lover, Come Back to Me" and "Body and Soul." My father said, "I wish you could have known your mother then." I knew that what he meant was back then she appeared beautiful and somehow innocent, and in need of rescue.

My father wanted to study botany. What he really wanted was to be a gardener, but he knew that was out of the question. His grandfather drove to the college and consulted with faculty. A history professor, whom Grandfather admired, told him, "Botany is not a course of study to be pursued by a gentleman." So Grandfather, sorrowfully, told my father that he would have to find some other profession. In discussions over dinner and on late afternoons in the potting shed and gardens behind Grandfather's house, they decided upon the law.

My father left for college when he was seventeen. He was six feet three inches and weighed more than 250 pounds. But from the first weeks as a college student, his fat drifted off. He forgot to eat. He gave away cookies and cakes that Mary sent by Railway Express. By the end of his sophomore year he weighed under 200 pounds. He had no idea why he quit eating and lost weight. "Just seemed to happen," he said.

When my father came home for vacations, he and my mother spent evenings together. They went to parties, where women who formerly saw Ham only as a friend-boy and not a boyfriend openly flirted. Was the girl who would become my mother in love with the young man who would become my father? No. Yes. She did not know. For one thing, she wanted a college degree, she didn't want to be dependent upon anyone ever, she didn't want to be poor. She wanted to be a singer. Not an opera singer, but a concertizing singer who travels on steamships and in private train cars and sings at Carnegie Hall in New York. She had favorites— Lotte Lehmann, Lily Pons, Rosa Ponselle, Marian Anderson. She listened to them on records. To save money for college she babysat, did housecleaning, and sang for weddings, funerals, and teas. She was always tired.

Soon my father was in his first year of law school in Fayetteville, Arkansas, and my mother was hundreds of miles away from home, a sophomore in college at a girls' school in Texas. She was also in deep trouble. In her hometown, anyone who wanted a solo sung at a wedding or funeral or spring tea simply said, "Well, we must ask Kathleen." She'd been paid, sometimes ten dollars, simply to stand in a pretty frock with her hair shining like a halo, and sing "In the Garden" or "Ave Maria" or "The Last Rose of Summer." At college, she felt ignorant, awkward, foolish. Her voice wasn't as full and well pitched as other students' voices, plus her teacher told her that she was a soprano, not, as she'd been taught, a contralto, like Marian Anderson. So she had worked all fall, lifting and increasing her range and brightening her tone. She waited tables and cleaned houses, anything to get money.

Ham and Kathleen were home for Christmas. My father said that my mother was so pathetic and that he loved her so much that he decided to try to elope. "Your mother," my father said to me on many occasions, "was a real beauty."

"Go in and get your coat right now," my father told

her on the afternoon before they were to leave for school, "and we'll run off and get married."

My mother said, no, no, she must return to college. My father kissed her and kissed her and she said, "Yes."

I want to tell them, "Stop, don't do it." You are going to be miserable and you are going to make everyone who knows you miserable. But I want to be born.

From photographs you can see that they were an attractive couple. Both were fair, their skin stretched pale over showy exotic blue veins; both were prone to freckling. Her hair was strawberry blonde; auburn highlights rolled across the thick wave that he brushed back from his broad forehead. My mother, even in the high heels that she favored, didn't stand much higher than my father's shirt pocket and she was tiny—perhaps 100 pounds, perhaps 105. "I looked," she said, many times over many years, "like his child, not his wife." She sounded angry when she said this.

They moved into my father's off-campus apartment. My mother enrolled in the undergraduate school. My mother had done enough cooking for herself and Carl that she could turn out breakfast, lunch, and dinner. She had, my father said, "a gift for pies and pie crusts." She made, he smiled as he enumerated, "berry pies of every kind and chocolate meringue, lemon meringue, coconut custard, cherry, rhubarb, apple and Dutch apple, chess, pecan, black bottom, peach, apricot, and raisin with sour cream." But her menus, my father said, reflected Carl's necessary penny-pinching. So my father wrote to Mary and asked if she would send recipes for pot roast, leg of lamb, lamb gravy, boiled Virginia ham, batter-fried chicken, Parker House rolls and devil's food cake.

My mother, years later, after the divorce, complained that no sooner were they married than my father got fat as a hog. He begged her, she said, to make pie, and she did. The next morning when she opened the pie safe, the pie tin was empty. She would expect to make roast beef hash from leftover chuck roast; when she peered into the refrigerator, she discovered that my father, in the middle of the night, had gobbled down meat, carrots, potatoes and onions, and left the dirty pan. One evening she found my father in the kitchen, boring a new hole in his belt with the ice pick.

My father admitted that this complaint about his behavior, unlike other complaints my mother had, was based on fact. "I did what she said I did," is how he put it. He agreed that he kept cupboards bare. His studies kept him up past midnight and he often ate all that remained from dinner. There was worse, he said, that my mother did not know. When he walked to school in the mornings, he stopped off in the German bakery and bought hot apple kuchen or raised doughnuts gritty with cinnamon sugar. On his way home he stopped at another bakery and bought chocolate éclairs. His expression turned ecstatic when he described those éclairs—"a lovely, thin chocolate icing and flaky pastry, but the best was the interior—the cool, egg custard."

Judith Moore

My father said that he was mortified that he couldn't stop eating. He said that he felt "under a strain." He had schoolwork and he had worries about what he should do after he graduated and about the war he felt would soon break out, any month, as the Germans commandeered acre after acre of Europe. My father confessed that he was somewhat afraid of my mother, who, he said, had turned out to be not all that pleasant a young woman with whom to live. She slammed doors when she was angry and she was angry often. She disliked his grand-parents and felt that they treated her with disdain (a grievance my mother aired with me), which, my father said, was not true. She felt that his grandparents spoiled him (another grievance my mother aired with me); my father felt that they loved him and that what most peo-ple regarded as love my mother regarded as "spoiling." My father detested my mother's mother, who had moved into Carl's cottage.

So, there were arguments about family. My parents, in their first years together, were largely supported by my father's grandparents and, my father said, there were ugly quarrels about money. My mother felt that my father was a spendthrift—that he subscribed to *Fortune* magazine she regarded as criminal. My father felt that my mother was a miser. My father reported that from the earliest days of marriage my mother threatened to leave him. He became inured to these threats, but he never figured that she wouldn't, one day, up and be gone.

In my father's last year of law school, he weighed

Fat Girl

250, maybe 260 pounds. My mother insisted he go to the campus infirmary and ask for help with a diet. Perhaps, she said, he had a glandular problem. He didn't. "Willpower," the doctor said. "It is a matter of willpower."

And then, as my father's last semester in law school opened, my mother's period did not start. She sat at the edge of the bed and sobbed. She couldn't keep anything down. She dropped out of school. Her life was ruined.

My father finished school that spring at the head of his class. He and my mother moved back to the little Oklahoma town where they had grown up. He took bar exams and was number one. Unlike many a man starting out, he didn't have to fret at getting clients; his grandfather made sure he would not sit idle. My father rented a first-floor office a block from his grandfather's bank. His name was painted on the window in gilt.

My father's grandparents had built my parents a house several blocks from their house. They moved in as soon as my father graduated. The house was white clapboard with a green, steeply pitched cottage roof and sat at one end of a half-block lot. Half the lot, nearest the house, ran down to the sidewalk in flawless lawn; the other half, beyond the lawn, was open soil, tilled and ready for a garden. "Our dream house," my father called it, adding, "Our architect friend designed it. He stippled in, by hand, with the tiniest of brushes, every inch of your wallpaper." The wallpaper was painted in repeat patterns of green strawberry plants, each red berry stippled with yellow "straw" of strawberry. My mother, when she recalled the house, also praised the

Judith Moore

beauty of the wallpaper. She, however, went on to criticize these strawberries as an example of my father's squandering of cash on luxuries.

Because my mother was pregnant and sickly, my grandparents sent Mary to stay in the spare bedroom. My mother was not thrilled with the arrangement. All that summer she took to her bed. But my father was happy to have Mary back. Mary, he said, did everything. She starched and ironed his shirts. She squeezed oranges for his breakfast juice. Bacon strips sizzled in the frying pan and brown eggs awaited his arrival at the breakfast table.

My mother was also not thrilled that Grammy, her mother, had moved in with Carl. She dreaded her mother's visit to the new house. She also felt angry and humiliated at my father's family's treatment of her mother. "From Day One," my mother said, years later, "they acted as if my mother did not exist. She was never invited to that house. And they had no use for me except as brood mare for their grandson. They tolerated me. That's all."

My father, also years later, laughed when I repeated my mother's complaints against his grandparents. He said his grandparents treated all the in-laws about the same as they treated my mother. For Thanksgiving, Christmas, Easter, he said, his grandmother seated all the "blood" at the long dining table and put those who'd married into the family at two round tables. "Actually," he added, "they treated your mother better. And, as for your mother's mother, of course they didn't have her in the house. Nobody did. Believe me, that old doll was persona non grata wherever she went."

When my father drove my mother to the hospital on the Saturday morning that I was born the nuns hustled her to bed and readied her. Hours passed. My father came and went, came and went. My mother sweat through one after another hospital gown. The nuns bathed her face. The doctor came and went. Finally, they put the ether cone over her nose and I was born, a breech birth. "You came out back-asswards," my mother will say when, later in life, I spill milk across the tablecloth or bump into an end table and set the crystal teardrops on the lamp trembling, "and you're still doing everything back-asswards now."

At the moment I entered the world my father was across the street from the delivery room at a delicatessen run by Germans. He was eating Muenster and headcheese and bratwurst and long pale strands of fresh kraut. When he leaned over to kiss my worn-out, weary mother, she tasted garlic and sour pickle and cabbage on his lips.

She would never forget this, never forgive it.

six

> "It's good when your conscience receives big
> wounds, because that makes it more
> sensitive to every twinge."

> —Kafka, Letter,
> January 27, 1904

What do I remember of those early years? Little. World War II was under way. Carl, although in his early forties, enlisted in the navy. When my father reported for his draft physical they would not take him: he was too fat.

My father was humiliated, he said, at being sent home from his physical as obese. Water diets, high-protein, all-vegetable and fruit—by this time my father had tried them all and had failed at them all. He had promised, before I was born, to lose fifty pounds. He lost twenty-five and then in the next three years he gained

Fat Girl

back all the twenty-five and added another thirty, maybe forty.

He was determined to lose weight. He hiked into the hills, carrying nothing but water and camping gear. He set up his tent, unrolled his bag, then his knees seemed to weaken. He panicked. What if he collapsed there, died? Leaving behind his gear, he walked and ran back to town, scattering rocks, falling, banging up a knee. He shook his head and laughed the laughter that is called "rueful" when he told me this story.

That my father was slender when they married and began to fatten soon after their elopement understandably left my mother feeling deceived. She married a thin man and ended up with a fat man. She decried what she called his "self-indulgence" with food and his physical laziness. Other than work in lawn and garden, which he enjoyed, she said he did nothing to help. He dealt with her complaints with sarcasm. "He talked to me," she said, "as if I were an idiot." And, she said frequently, over many years, "He used me like a doormat. He *walked* on me."

I also used her like a doormat and walked all over her. I wrecked her life. My mother told me many times that once she gave birth to me, she was trapped. She also said that I tore her up down there, that after my enormous butt pushing its way out of her, she was never the same.

My mother had many complaints: about my father's desire for what she felt was "perverse" sex (what now we call "blow jobs," which she felt was a sign that he was homosexual); that he "lacked ambition," that he never exerted himself to make money. She said that he turned away clients, for no reason other than he didn't like them. She said he was the world's worst snob (he was).

They fought over me. His grandparents spoiled me. Mary spoiled me. I had more toys than any child could play with and more clothes than a child could wear. They fought about Grammy. My father didn't want her in the house. He didn't like what he characterized as her "rough talk." He didn't like the way she treated Mary. He didn't like the way she got my mother upset. He said—and my mother later agreed—that Grammy wished to break up my parents' marriage because she couldn't stand to see her so well-off. My mother, in the rare moments when she became weepy, was wont to say, "If it hadn't been for my mother, your father and I would still be married."

(I had to talk to many people about this next period in my parents' lives, the time immediately before their separation. They had always been such a mystery, my mother and father—why they married, why they broke up. So I queried my father, my mother, my uncle Carl and his friend Mr. Huffman, my paternal grandfather's fourth wife, and most recently an old friend of my mother's. I acquired copies of papers my mother's lawyer prepared when my mother filed for divorce. From those documents and from what these people told me, I reconstructed certain events.)

Fat Girl

I know that it was midsummer and hot and that the war was going poorly for the Allies. I know that my father was growing a Victory Garden of ambitious size. (During World War II vegetable gardens were grown all across the United States to raise food for families, friends, and neighbors. Gardeners and their families canned and dried produce for winter and ate it fresh, of course, in spring and summer. These gardens enabled more supplies to be shipped to our troops around the world.) My mother had returned to school and had finished her bachelor's degree in music and had begun graduate work.

In the weeks before my parents separated, my father was in the midst of a strenuous diet given him by the family doctor. When he told this story, he remembered that this diet consisted of many grapefruit, which, he said, were supposed to shrink your stomach. He explained that much emphasis was put in those days on shrinking the stomach. In addition to the diet, he was taking Benzedrine, given him by the doctor as a diet aid. My father knew nothing about Benzedrine. All he knew was that he felt hungry and crazy and that night after night he couldn't sleep.

On what would be my father's final night in the house where we lived for four years, he was sweating. The fan blades clacked. He was thinking about green peas and red-jacketed new potatoes, brave new world explorers, setting sail through a butter-dappled white sauce. Out of nowhere, pheasants he fried once in a South Dakota hunting camp over an open fire spread themselves out on a blue speckled tin plate. Feral mysterious gravy draped the peaked breasts. Food, he said, called loudly to him that night. He felt sure that he went through a long menu of meats and vegetables and fruits and salads and desserts.

He thought that had he not been taking Benzedrine, what happened next might not have happened. He eased out of bed and left the bedroom. The doctor suggested that when my father felt hungry that he drink warm water with lemon juice squeezed in it or eat celery and carrot sticks. In the kitchen my father opened the refrigerator door. What he found was the pint Mason jar of ice water filled with celery and carrots sticks.

My father could not remember what mental events led him to close the refrigerator door and open the door into the garage and walk down the concrete steps into the garage. The Packard was parked outside. On one wall of the garage, my father stored his rake, hoes, spades and shovels and his fishing vest. Fishing, he said, always gave him more pleasure than did hunting. But hunting was one activity he could engage in with his father without quarrels breaking out. So he hunted with his father (who would hunt, on foot, until he died at eighty-five). My father's Parker twelve-gauge side-by-side double-barreled shotgun rested on the top shelf.

My father said that he was sure that he felt reckless, that he was crazy from the pills. He took down the shotgun, no doubt admiring the blue steel double barrel, the ornately checkered Circassian walnut stock that gave him a good grip even when his hands turned clammy on him. The gun was heavy—maybe six pounds—but so well balanced it didn't feel that way.

He reached into a box and pulled out four shells and dropped them into his bathrobe pocket. The shells, I think, would have made the pocket droop. He walked back through the house, gun hanging from his right hand, safety under his thumb.

He turned Mary's doorknob and let himself into her darkened room. Mary sat straight up in the bed, hand to her mouth. He, of course, was carrying the gun.

"Mary," my father whispered, "I was wondering if you could possibly make me a lemon meringue pie."

My father felt sure that Mary wore some sort of voluminous nightgown and a head wrap. He recalled being in the kitchen with Mary and her trying to dissuade him from pie. "Maybe," he said, "she suggested an early breakfast."

But he told her, "Lemon pie." He felt terrible, he said, because he had frightened her. I tried to see this as my father talked. Mary would have lit the gas oven with a wooden match. The gas would have whooshed. She would get Crisco, flour, Morton salt. She would take out her glass mixing bowl, her pastry blender. My father was sure that he sat at the breakfast table. He was sure he set the shotgun on the table.

Mary, my father said, never measured pie crust ingredients. She did it by feel, as did my father. Mary would have filled the double boiler with water and set the water boiling. She would have pared lemon rind, juiced lemons, broken eggs—expertly separating whites into a big bowl, yolks into a smaller one. The curtains in that kitchen were made of bright yellow cotton printed with red chickens. These curtains would have framed the darkness where the backyard Victory Garden stood. The scent of lemon and baking crust would have drifted across the kitchen. Mary would have stirred with a long-handled wooden spoon the egg yolk, sugar, lemon juice and lemon rind, the dollop of butter for the lemon filling.

My father said that he knew for sure that Mary asked him to put the shotgun back in the garage. He said that he was on his way to do that very thing when my mother walked in. When she saw the shotgun, my father said she screamed like a banshee.

That morning, my father ate his lemon meringue pie, then showered and dressed for work. My mother didn't speak to him. As soon as she saw his shoulders pass through the line of poplars that provided a windbreak for the yard and garden, she telephoned her mother. She told her what happened. In no time at all Grammy appeared at the front door.

I remember the next part myself, and that is that my mother and Grammy packed my father's Hickey Freeman worsteds and cotton seersuckers, his prewar Brooks Brothers shirts, green-striped pajamas and boxer shorts into suitcases and boxes and bags. They set the suitcases and boxes and bags on the back stoop. What I didn't know at the time, I learned later from my mother and my father and Uncle Carl, was that my mother set

Fat Girl

her diaphragm on top of one of the suitcases. What I also didn't know was that my mother wrote my father a note saying that his uncle, also a lawyer, would be getting in touch, that she was getting a divorce, that he was a dangerous man who could not be permitted near the child or herself.

That day when my mother threw my father out, I was going on four and I wasn't fat. Photographs taken of me before the break show a beautiful, effervescent red-haired child. When I get out the basket where I keep photographs I am surprised how happy I look. I am surprised as I look through photos how busy I am—my playmate Janet and I chase a white kitten through green grass, I stand at the kitchen table with Mary and she hands me folded white napkins. Again in the kitchen with Mary I am snapping green beans, I dig in the garden, I pull a red wagon (the wagon in the old Kodak has faded to a rusty red). "That's the biggest smile," I say, touching my almost-four-year-old face. I say, to that face, "You are so cute!"

After the divorce, my father took off and my mother left me with Grammy, who by then had settled on a forty-acre farm in Arkansas that she bought with money Uncle Carl had given her. My father went to Chicago and my mother to the Eastman School of Music in Rochester, New York, to get a master's degree in applied music. She remained determined to become a singer.

Grammy was sixty-five when I went to live with her. I see her clearly as she was then—short and fat, her frothy white hair wild around her head. Her skin hangs in folds off her square jawline. Her dentures shift in her mouth when she smiles, which she does not do often. Her lips gather like a coin purse around the dentures.

When Grammy shopped or visited lady friends she wore close-fitting rayon dresses and Red Cross shoes with sensible one-and-one-half-inch heels. Under the dresses her corset stays showed. To work on the farm, and she worked hours as long as those of her two hired hands (two elderly men named Bushels and Buckles), she wore housedresses she sewed from flour sacks printed with flowers and rubber boots that rose to her knees. Her breasts drooped down over her round stomach and her "bee-hind," as she called buttocks, rode behind her, living a jiggling life of its own. She hated my father. She minced no words. My father was my "no-good, spoiled, rich-kid father." I was "his spitting image," she said, waggling her butcher knife so close to my nose my eyes crossed.

Grammy was repulsive to me, and when she got near me I connived to move away. I hated the way she smelled—like soured washcloths—and the way she looked—angry.

I turned sullen and disagreeable. I turned mean. I tried without success to make friends with Grammy's black-and-white speckled hens, and when they would not let me pet them I taught her mangy farm dog to bring them down. I screamed, "Sic 'em, sic 'em!" He grabbed the squawking hens between his teeth. Their squirming and pecking excited him. He growled. He worried their necks. When a hen ceased flapping, he dropped her and loped away to sprawl in the shade. I felt a disorienting pleasure as I watched the dog tear at a hen. Once the dog walked away, I promised myself I would never do this again. I would try to erase what I'd done from my mind.

Grammy was mystified each time she found a mauled hen. Then one afternoon she caught me siccing the hound on a pretty pullet. She grabbed my hair and she slapped my face and boxed my ears. She tore a branch off a forsythia bush and switched my bare arms and bare legs until my arms and legs were covered with bloody stripes. She was always hitting me and screaming at me.

I don't blame her, even now, for how she treated me. She was a fat, tired, disappointed, desperate and lonely old woman who suffered with stomach pains, which must have been some form of colitis. In the drawer of the library table that stood in her living room she kept pamphlets on diseases of the colon; these pamphlets, together with Jehovah's Witness leaflets, were part of the material from which I learned to read.

Uncle Carl, by then, was on a warship in the Pacific and Grammy was afraid he'd be killed in the war and never come home. She worried, she said, day and night and day.

She hated me. I hated her. I was not good company. I tracked in mud, left doors open. I let the farmhouse fill with flies and mosquitoes, smeared dirty hands on walls and dresses, broke drinking glasses. When Grammy's broad short back was turned, I stuck out my tongue. More than once I told her I hated her, and most of the time I did.

Grammy was the first person I saw naked, although I did not try to see her naked. On summer evenings, after a bath, she walked around the farmhouse with everything showing. The corset she wore during the day would have cut red vertical ridges into her rib cage, her belly and upper thighs. Her long loose breasts—she called them "dinners"—were striped with stretch marks and tipped with long beige nipples; the breasts fell down over rolls of fat that hung between her hips. The lowest roll of fat sat along her thighs. Between her thighs, at the vee of her sex, were a small number of yellow-white hairs, and beneath the sparse outcrop of hair, drooping purple labia. Her buttocks had the same clabber look as her thighs. If she didn't call her bottom her "bee-hind" she called it her "hind end," as if her body were a hog or a steer and she was talking to the butcher about what cuts of meat she wanted herself chopped into.

Grammy worked unbelievably hard, especially when you consider that she was sixty-five and vastly over-weight. Year-round, dawn and dusk, she milked, and she milked without machines, rubbing the cows' udders afterward with Bag Balm. She ran the milk separator and she churned butter (she traded and sold milk and eggs and butter). She shoveled out manure and spread fresh hay in the barn, she watered and fed cows, chick-ens, horses, mules, and slopped the hogs. She helped pregnant cows deliver their young. Once spring came

Fat Girl

she had the garden, the canning, the baby chicks mailed to her from the hatchery, and the piglets. When all that was done, she would come in, sighing, through the screened-in back porch, swearing about Bushels or Buckles or a cow, a mule, a calf, the war, or me. She would pull off her rubbers and tie on her apron and begin housework—the laundry, ours and the hands', and the cooking and baking and the cleaning up.

My grandmother's butcher knives left me with a terror of knives. Even now, her knives furnish my nightmares. She honed them so often that the blades wore in the middle and looked a bit like scimitars. During the two years I lived with her, I saw her castrate a horse, slit throats on squealing Chester White and black-and-white Poland China hogs, and with her short-handled axe chop heads off unwieldy turkeys and a nation of chickens. She was the Nazi of the barnyard, entirely businesslike in these procedures, and it seemed not to bother her when blood soaked her apron and blood dried in splotches on her bare arms and legs and in the folds of her neck. "If you want to eat you got to kill," she said, when I ran in fright from her.

I was often sick. Boils broke out across my stomach and I ran fevers and I put my head down in the toilet bowl and vomited and sobbed and choked. I missed my mother and I missed my father and I missed Mary and I missed Janet and I missed my house and my room with the red strawberries. But mostly, I grew "big," Grammy said, "as Man Mountain Dean." I never knew who Man Mountain Dean was. I assumed that he was a monster who opened his vast gutted mouth so wide that it ached and then ran down mountains, and while he ran he ate every tree, every house, every horse, cow, mother hog and piggies, boar and goat and sheep and bleating lamb that got in his way. That's who Man Mountain Dean was.

Lord knows, I chowed down on Grammy's cooking. She served up to me and to her hired hands three meals a day plus snacks. She fed us bacon and eggs, sausage patties, strawberry jam, butter-soaked hot biscuits, molasses-sopped flapjacks, fried chicken, baked hams, thick pork chops, puffy dumplings, potato pancakes, homemade egg noodles, mashed potatoes, apple and cherry pies and three-layer coconut cakes and huckleberry and peach and boysenberry cobblers, crisp gingerbread cookies, Kadota figs afloat in clotted cream, cows' thick milk and the butter she churned from that milk.

I got my elbows up on the kitchen table and I fed my face. I ate and ate and ate. I starved for my father, whom I would never once see for many years, and my mother, who came to visit for Christmas and soon again was gone. I ate Grammy's fried chicken and Grammy's cobbler because they tasted good and because I was trying to fill up the grave my father and my mother had dug for me.

When I asked Grammy, "When is Mama coming?," if she answered me at all, she said, equably, "I don't know," or, angrily, "If she gets married again, her new husband may not want you." Once she was reading a letter from my mother and looked out at me over the top of her spectacles and said, "Your mama has a soldier boy." I hardly dared think of my father. He was bad. I was like him.

I was young. I did not know what would come to me, I did not know what rules would be violated, what laws ignored. Already my heart was broken and I did not know it.

seven

"Do not be afraid of yourself.
You are the world."

—Langston Hughes,
Life of Langston Hughes, Volume II

I was ready to start first grade when my mother plucked me up from the farm and carried me off to New York. I'd forgotten her face. I don't think I could have picked her out of a crowd. I do not recall how I felt at seeing her again. She'd been gone too long.

I was fat. Not quite six and so fat you could hardly find my blue eyes, squished as they were between my fat cheeks and fat forehead. Yes, even my forehead was fat. So were my feet. My feet were so fat that when my mother took me to Best's across the street from St.

Fat Girl

Patrick's Cathedral for school shoes the man who measured my feet said they were too fat for girls' brown oxfords. I had to be fitted in boys' shoes. My mother didn't look at me, and with the shoe man she acted as if I were not her little girl but somebody else's. When we left Best's and walked out onto busy Fifth Avenue she squeezed my upper arm hard and hissed that she was going to put me on a reducing diet, starting that minute.

My mother was dainty and petite. She wore a size five shoe and a size six dress and her bra was 34-B; when she slipped her stocking feet into her high-heeled slippers, she was five feet tall. She was built like a pear, with a pear's waist and rounded hips. Her voluptuous bosom sat high on her chest; the crevasse between her breasts was deep and she powdered there. She did not yet have the enlarged rib cage that more years of voice lessons would give her. But she already had the voice of an angel that floated through rooms where we lived. She already was singing, "Can you see but a white lily grow, before rude hands have touched it?"

In the days when I first came to live with her in her rooms in Brooklyn, she wore her auburn hair in what I think of as a World War II pompadour. The hair was pulled up off her lovely heart-shaped face with tortoise-shell combs, one comb tucked in back of each ear. Atop her head, which always seemed overlarge for her delicate frame, she piled the hair high. When light hit the auburn strands just right, you could see gold among it. She had one of those slow, rhythmic hip-swaying walks. Her three-inch heels clicked along floors and sidewalks. When we walked to the subway and down subway stairs, men turned to stare at her musical behind.

The city frightened me. What I was used to were cows and weeping willows and red hens and muddy pink swine and stillness broken by my grandmother's guttural mutter, by the cows' low moans, by the radio playing war news and President Roosevelt speeches and hillbilly music. That's what they called it then, "hillbilly," not "country and western."

I flinched against the noise, soot, and the fast-moving crowds. Puerto Ricans, Negroes, Orientals and any male of any color with a pencil mustache frightened me. I grabbed for my mother's hand. She said, "You're breaking my hand. Don't hold on so tight, for God's sake." She shook me off.

The first year I was in New York a lot of snow fell and summer was hot and I got bad colds and sick stomachs and stayed home many days from school and threw up into a tin saucepan that my mother used to warm Campbell's soup. Mama put me on a reducing diet, which was head lettuce and dry diet toast and soft-boiled eggs and hamburger patties and no butter and no dessert. She wouldn't let me take school lunch and I longed for those lunches. I liked school foods that everyone else hated, the meatballs that tasted faintly of dog food and the cereal hot dogs and the shepherd's pie topped with mashed potatoes that were browned underneath a broiler, the pie itself filled with lamb and olive-green canned peas, the peas mealy and faded in

Fat Girl

color, and orange carrot cubes, the carrot color also dulled.

No matter whether I cheated or didn't cheat, I didn't get thin and was always hungry and always trying to steal nickels from Mama's purse so I could stop at the candy store on the way to school and buy a Peter Paul Mounds bar, which had chocolate over moist milky coconut. This candy store stood on a corner. The store sold newspapers, magazines, comic books and penny candy and candy bars. Glass jars held juice-filled paraffin lips and jawbreakers and orange and lemon slices and horehound drops. Racks were stacked with Life-Savers and Charms, with Baby Ruth, Bit-O-Honey, Chuckles, Milk Duds, Milky Way, Almond Joy, 5th Avenue, Heath Bar, M&M's, Oh Henry, Reese's Peanut Butter Cups, Sky Bar, 3 Musketeers, Tootsie Roll and Sugar Babies. Comic books were displayed in racks. Each month a new issue emerged with stories of Porky Pig, Archie and Jughead and Veronica, of Donald Duck and his nephews Huey and Louie and his uncle, the miserly Scrooge McDuck. Donald and his family were my favorites.

I dreaded schooldays. I talked funny and dropped my *g*'s and boys and girls in my class called me "hillbilly." I tried to make friends and didn't. When we had fire drills our teacher lined us up two by two and I walked alone at the end of the line. Nobody was really mean, at least not yet. For the most part, they didn't even look at me. I might as well have been air.

My memory of that year is mostly blank. I was waking up from the long sleep of living with my grand-mother on her dark ramshackle farm, where I talked with chickens and the stinking mangy farm dog and the graceful huge-eyed heifers. I was waking up from living far out in the country where sounds were *cluck* and *whinny* and *moo* and *oink*. I began, bit by bit, to open my eyes. I thought that with my mother my real life was beginning. The years before were waiting. Waiting for Mama to come for me.

I thought that I should be happy, living with my mother. I wasn't. I wasn't happy at all. The longer my mother had been gone, the kinder the mother I built in my mind became. She blew softly across my wounds and painted them stinging orange with the glass Mer-curochrome wand. When I emptied my milk glass, she filled that glass again. When night came, she bathed me with a soap that smelled sweet; she dried me tenderly, buffed me down with warm terry cloth; she gently lifted my flannel nightie down over my head, careful to not disturb my curls. She cradled me in her arms and sang me lullabies and her voice was as beautiful as birds' twilight songs. But when we finally were together in her Brooklyn apartment, my mother was not anything like the mother I made up for myself. She screamed and she yelled, she stomped her feet. She told me shut up, shut up.

I was always behind her, saying, "Mama, Mama." I stepped on her heels. She said, "You are eating me alive." I understand now that she felt devoured by me. This cannot have been easy.

Fat Girl

What I see this afternoon when I am older than my mother was when we lived in Brooklyn is that not only did I want more than my mother had to give but that I missed my father. I do not think I so much missed the man who was my father as I wanted a father. Why I say this is that I do not think that consciously I remembered my father. What I knew about him I learned from Mama and her mother. They said, "You give him an inch and he takes a mile." I learned that he had a new wife and a new child, a son. My mother when she was mad said no wonder I was bad, what with his blood that ran in me. She said I was the spitting image of him, that I had his sulky lower lip.

I worried about this. I worried that because of my father's blood I might have been born bad. Underneath the yellow fat made from so many gravies and cherry pies and apple crisps under thick cream, so much toast buttered and jellied, so many deep sunset-yellow egg yolks, I imagined that the bad Tootsie Roll Pop filling of me seethed and simmered. I thought about the electric chair that they kept at Sing Sing. I was afraid I'd end up in the electric chair, what we called the "hot seat" back then.

There were the years when children teased me and I had few friends and my clothes were tight and Mama put me on one reducing diet after another. My clothes were either made at home on Mama's Singer or bought in the chubby section at Best's or Macy's or Gimbel's. Clerks in the chubby section had pulled dresses over many an ungainly fat girl and tried to fit her into garments that made her look pretty to her parents and to herself. But they knew the hopelessness of it all. The tight-bodiced dresses worn by girls who were rod thin could not be worn by a fat girl. I wanted pastels and plaids and prints; I wanted wide and gathered skirts. I wanted ruffles, I longed for skirts I could twirl. What I wore were navy blues and browns.

That's what it was like to be a fat girl. But that's not all, that's not even the worst or biggest part of it. Being a fat girl was as much about wanting more than my mother had to give me and about wanting my father, not having a father at all. I cannot pull the stories apart; they reach out for each other; they grab on and bite down. They hold tight to each other. I imagine passengers aboard a sinking ship, grasping each other for dear life, and think that the story of my fatness and the story of my longing grasp each other for dear life.

Between first and second grade I spent the summer with Grammy on her farm in Arkansas. When Mama came for me before Labor Day she was furious. I was barefoot and dressed in denim overalls. Not only had I gained back the weight I'd lost, I'd added more. Nothing fit, not even my underwear. My mother set up Grammy's sewing machine in the living room. She sewed me several outfits to wear on the train back to New York. While she pumped up and down on the sewing machine treadle and the sweat ran down her beautiful and weary heart-shaped face, she said how disgusted she was with me and with Grammy. When I stood close to her so she could measure my waist or pin up the hem to my dress, she pinched me hard and

Fat Girl

flicked me with her fingernail and hissed again and again how disgusted she was. She said I looked ugly and that boys and girls at my school would keep on teasing me. She said second grade would be like first grade and I would not make friends.

She said nobody wanted to be friends with a fat girl.

My body felt like burdens I was carrying on my back. I felt like a field animal. I touched my fat arms and felt surprise that I had not grown fur. I was not human. I wrote that down sometimes in my lined notebooks: I am a wild animal. I had been raised by wolves or wild Indians. I lived in burrows. I was dirty. I did not know about knives and forks and spoons. I dug roots. I picked berries. I killed rabbits with rocks. I ate the rabbits half raw and rabbit blood sluiced down my chin onto my bare chest. I shat and peed right on the ground. I did not wipe myself afterward.

Even though I was too old for the story (I was six going on seven) I still liked the three little pigs. I liked to consider their trio of houses—straw, wood and brick. Straw would catch fire and wood could be blown down. Brick was what I built my house with, I thought, and now I see the building materials were the yellow fat bricks.

The clean pink picture-book pigs were nothing like real pigs that grunted in their pen on my grandmother's farm. I dwelt on the difference between the book pigs and my grandmother's filthy swine. Book pigs smiled. Rather than the squinting eyes from which real pigs looked out at you meanly, book pigs had wide blue

Shirley Temple eyes. Real pigs, if you fell down in their pen and no one was around, would eat you alive. I ran this scenario through my mind more than once. There I was, dressed in a summer dress, a pair of the Mary Janes I had yet to own and white anklets trimmed with lace. I climbed up onto a slat on the fence and offered the pigs an ear of corn. The corn was bright yellow. I slipped and fell into the mud. The hogs surrounded me. They ran their snouts up my bare calf. They ripped off my blue skirt. I screamed. I howled. Sometimes the pigs ate me alive and left nothing in their wallow but the shreds of my dress and a bright buckle from the Mary Janes. I could not imagine what happened after they ate me except that I could see bits of me in their stomachs, the same way that I could see Jonah floating inside the Bible whale.

When I started second grade in PS 169 in Brooklyn, I weighed 112 pounds. Were I to show you the photographs that survive those years, you would see a child who looks like a short fat housewife. "Matronly" is what my mother said about how I looked. Only the small hands and the full moon face would tell you that this photograph I handed you is a photograph of a child.

I don't know how tall I was, but certainly I was a normal height. I weighed ten pounds more than my mother. I got out of breath when I walked up hills. My thighs rubbed together when I walked; friction rubbed my skin raw and the perspiration, raised by fear, a chemically powerful terror sweat, literally rubbed salt in my skin's wounds. A tropic humid climate, directly below my hairless chubby pudenda, formed under my skirts and kept the skin damp along my inner thighs. Open sores festered on the inside of each thigh. The pain was so bad when I walked that to keep from crying out I counted down from 100 or said the Lord's Prayer or what I could recall of the Twenty-third Psalm. I knew this psalm because Grammy taught me to say, after her, "The Lord is my shepherd, I shall not want."

I was the only fat girl in the class. Nobody was even chubby. One girl in our class got out early some afternoons because she was a model. What she modeled were girls' dresses and she also modeled, she said, with toys and food and restaurants. Once she told us this I was on the lookout for her picture in the advertisements in the subway. She was popular with girls and with boys, and she was popular with me. I loved to look at her. Her name was Margie, a name not uncommon then. Every day for lunch she ate a lettuce and tomato sandwich on white bread and an apple. She sighed when she ate and she looked weary, as if eating were a job, which for her I guess it was.

In second grade I already wore teachers'-sized blue cotton gym bloomers. These bloomers were a one-piece romper suit. The legs of the suit ended at the same spot shorts end. My behind filled out the pants. The legs of these uniforms were finished with strong elastic. The elastic even on teachers' uniforms was not long enough to circle comfortably around my fat thighs. The elastic bit into my fat. On either side of the elastic, my soft flesh bulged up. As the phys ed hour progressed the elastic bit harder and harder. Some days, depending on which uniform I was given for the week, the elastic bit in so far that my flesh cut open and bled. The pain was awful. I didn't dare pay the elastic any mind because the other girls and our teacher would see me doing it and they would know that I was doing it because of the tightness and that the tightness was because of the fatness.

When I was in first grade no one paid much attention to me. I was occasionally teased. Mostly, I was ignored. No one talked to me at lunch and rarely did anyone allow me to join in a game at recess. Right away, in second grade, a group of older boys took after me. Out on the playground, after lunch, they circled me. They yelled, "Fat girl! Fat girl! Fat girl!" They sang, "I don't want her, you can have her, she's too fat for me." I saw the hairs in their noses, they got that close. I smelled boy BO.

The meanest was Dean, who every day wore brown plaid pants. He was the showoff of the bunch and he put his hands on his hips like a dancer and wriggled back and forth while he sang "I don't want her, you can have her, she's too fat for me." The others sang with him, off-key in pure boy soprano.

I never knew what to do. I stood and stared while their mouths opened and shut, while the hard dentals of "don't" and the soft labial "you" spit and slid from their mouths. They had baby teeth missing. We all did. Wide gaps where our square rabbit teeth would soon drop down.

Fat Girl

Rodney, who was one of the most hateful boys, especially liked to poke a finger in my rear end, which in Brooklyn they called your heinie. He was a fourth-grader. He would breathe right down on me and stick a finger right between my buttocks and push and push. He had liver lips and his breath gave off a bubble-gum smell. He would put his liver lips right on my ear. One day he said the worst thing to me. He said, "I bet you'd eat my shit." Rodney also would come up to me on the playground and push me against the chain-link fence. When he got me pushed hard against the fence he would rub his hands over my huge stomach and ask me, "You got a baby in there, Fatso?"

Other times Rodney put his hand over my mouth and crushed my lips against my teeth and with his other hand touched the area between my legs that Grammy had called my "business." Finally one day I got my mouth open and bit his hand. He slapped me hard and said, "Maybe your ma should put a dog muzzle on you."

I told no one. I said not one word about my chafed thighs, about Rodney and his friends.

The fatness was my problem.

eight

"Think of your head as an unsafe
neighborhood; don't go there alone."

—Augusten Burroughs,
Dry

I loved Bing Crosby. I loved his nickname, "Der Bingle."
When I listened to his program on the radio I made believe that Bing Crosby was my father. I knew though
that he wasn't and I knew better, when people asked me
what my father did, than to say, "Oh, he's a singer on
the radio. He's Bing Crosby." I also loved big trees and
I scratched against tall tree trunks and made believe
that their rough bark was my father's skin.

Once, after I listened to Bing Crosby sing "Blue
Moon" on his Bing Crosby hour, I asked Mama if she

was in love with my father when they got married. Before Mama even had time to answer, I asked a second question. I asked, "Was it love at first sight?"

Mama sat in her easy chair, her feet up on the footstool. She was letting down a hem in my navy blue jumper to make room for my most recent height and girth. She was picking out the old stitches with her needle. I was scared of needles. Mama stood up fast and threw the jumper down to the carpet and got her face right down into my face and screamed, "Don't you dare poke around in my affairs, Sister Sue."

I also asked her, back then, where my father lived. She would only say, "Far away." I asked her if I would see him again and she said, "No." She said he was "no good" and "lazy" and that I was disloyal and ungrateful to ask about him. She said that if I went to live with my father and his new wife that his new wife would make me scrub floors.

I watched fathers and their little girls. I watched them on the subway, sitting next to each other on the straw seats. One Saturday morning on the way with Mama to Manhattan, where she went to take her voice lesson, I watched a father remove from his daughter's hands her gloves and tuck them into his overcoat pocket. The girl, perhaps a year younger than was I, leaned against her father's side. She fell asleep. She had those thin eyelids that you can almost see through and the eyelids flickered while she slept. I watched fathers and daughters when from school we went on a field trip to the Metropolitan Museum to see van Gogh's paintings. The father and daughter duo whom I clearly recall held hands as they ascended the museum staircase. She had long brunette braids, each tied with a red ribbon; the ribbons bounced on the back of her coat. She slipped, the little girl did, on the stairs and banged her knee and howled and her father scooped her up in his arms and knelt there as we walked around them.

What cut me deepest was when we went to the Macy's Thanksgiving Day Parade. Grammy was visiting and she wanted to go and we did. What I saw there were little girls riding on their fathers' shoulders; they had their hands around their fathers' necks and they threw back their heads and they wriggled and laughed. I would break a father's shoulders, I thought. I would break his neck. All his bones would crackle underneath my big hind end.

Nobody lifted me up. I imagined what it would be like to be lifted up and twirled like Cyd Charisse got twirled. I wanted to be a ballet dancer and when I so foolishly said to Grammy and Mama that's what I wanted, Grammy guffawed, an ugly guffaw where she opened her mouth so wide that I could see all the way down to her gullet. I could see her long uvula quiver. Mama laughed too. She said I'd break off my feet if I tried to stand on my toes, because what I was was her baby elephant.

Another thing Mama said was, "Keep your hands to yourself, do you hear me?" Were I able to recover, minute by minute, my childhood, I believe that we could count on fingers and toes and not use up, say, my left foot's stubby digits, how many times my mother kissed me. She must have occasionally pecked my cheek. I know, however, that she never with any regularity put an arm around me and gave a parental hug. She did not smile down on me, lighting me the way noon sun lights pastures. I do not remember her saying to me as someone, years later, did, "You are the apple of my eye." On that occasion, this apple-of-the-eye declaration caused me to dissolve into grateful tears. I knew at that very moment, sitting at a table in an old hotel that looked out onto a park, that I had waited all my life to be the apple of someone's eye. My mother never said that, nor anything like that, to me. She said, "You make me sick, just to look at you." She said, when she got ready to whip me and raised the brown leather belt and I cowered at her feet, "I am going to cut the blood out of you."

Each month or so when the teacher marched the class to the nurse's room to be weighed I was terrified. I dreaded this day. You never knew when it was going to happen, either, so you couldn't stay home sick. As each child stood on the scale, one nurse pulled out the bar that measured height. I heard the bar clank. As soon as the nurse got the bar atop the child's head, the nurse called out the height—four feet five inches, whatever— and the second nurse penciled in the measurement. Then the weigh-in nurse slid back and forth the bar on the scale. When the weight settled, she called out, "Seventy-one pounds, Marie Tagliavia." The nurse penciled that in.

Not one other child in that entire class needed the

one-hundred-pound bar. I knew that. As the line grew shorter, as child after child was measured and weighed, he or she went to stand at the back of the room. "Don't fidget," the teacher might say, or, "No talking. Shhh."

I wanted to bolt. I couldn't. I bowed my head, I gazed at my boy's FFFF-width brown oxfords. I kept count as one after another child got weighed. I hoped the A-bomb would fall or a fire start before the nurse got to me.

One thing that worried me about being fat was what I would do if the apartment caught fire and a fireman came to save me and I was too fat to carry. Or if they had a fire at school and the firemen climbed in the windows to carry out children and save them from the licking flames and here I was so fat that nobody volunteered to save me. I could hear my fat sizzle and snap the way pork chops sizzle and snap in the skillet. The next day when they sorted through the burned-down school, they would find my bones and when somebody asked, "Whose bones are those?," one fireman who was there would say, "I bet that's that fat girl who was too heavy to carry out the window and down the ladder to safety."

When I stood on the scale, the scale jiggled. Boys and girls near me were laughing and the teacher said "Shhh" again. "One hundred and ten, almost one hundred and eleven," the nurse who weighed me called out to the nurse who jotted in your weight.

Before we left the infirmary the nurse who weighed me handed me a note for my mother. She said that she

Fat Girl

wrote that maybe I had a bad thyroid and she should take me to the family doctor. We didn't have a family doctor. We didn't have a family.

I wanted a family. On soft pulpy postwar notebook paper I drew a house. Then I cut the house into one section about one-third in size and the other section two-thirds. I put my father and his new wife and his new child into the larger area, which had a living room and dining room and upstairs bedrooms and bathrooms and a wide brick fireplace in which I colored orange flames flickering up from logs. Except that my mother said that my father was fat like me and that he was more than six feet tall, I did not know what he looked like. So I drew a tall stick figure with a round belly. I drew his wife little, because Mama and Grammy said that his new wife looked like Mama. I had her carry the baby in her stick arms. I wrapped the baby in a blue blanket. That baby was who my father loved.

In our side of the house we had the kitchen and one bedroom and one bathroom and radiators that clinked in the morning when the super turned on the furnace. There was me, a stick figure with rotund belly and wide hips, and little Mama. I put her in a dress onto which I drew the tiniest flowers I could draw with a number-three pencil. I opened her mouth wide and drew notes coming out of it. I was passionate about pencil lead points and liked to keep mine sharp.

I wanted Daddy, Mama and me. I wanted to walk between them, holding each of their hands. His hand was substantial and his palm square and his fingers easily enclosed my hand. Her hand was cool and slender and her fingers held mine lightly and she used her other hand to reach down and smooth my curls. I looked up at her and she shone down on me with the light that shines down from Mary in museum paintings. Gold framed us. I skipped between them. Above me, they chatted, bantered, and occasionally they said to me, "We're almost there, darling." Or, "honey," or, "precious." I stuffed my mouth with delicious love names they called me. I was their "little girl."

All the while that I craved the implied sweetness of words like "little girl" I thought I was a monster. My family had already dug my grave, yes. An emptiness more still than that in which you hear pins drop grew inside me. I was fattening on a dry wind. My badness grew. I knew I was worse than anyone. Every time Mama slapped me so hard my ears rang or that Grammy knocked me one with the straw broom I knew I deserved every blow. When my mother castigated me for wearing her out by causing her to beat me, deep in my heart I agreed. I see her now, not that sweet pretty Mama of the Mom and Dad fantasy, but a madwoman, her heart-shaped face as wild as the face of a Greek tragedienne. She wept with fury. I was that fury's cause. She said that. Then she said, "Aren't you ashamed of yourself? You with a face not even a mother could love. You."

I was. I am.

People said when I was a child that inside every fat person a thin person longed to pop out. I did not believe

Fat Girl

that. I believed that inside every fat person was a hole the size of the world; I believed that every fat person wanted to fill that hole by eating the world. It wasn't enough to eat food. You had to swallow air, you had to chew up everyone who got near you. No wonder, I thought, that nobody liked me or liked me all that much. I was like the wild animals in my *Homes and Habitats of Wild Animals* book who spent their lives hunting down other animals and eating them raw. Nobody much liked me, I thought, because they sensed that I wanted to bite into their bare arms and bare cheeks and rip off chunks of them and chew and chew and swallow. I wanted to eat them not because they looked particularly tasty or even because I was hungry, but because I was empty and I needed to feel full.

I built walls of fat, and I lived inside. When those boys said fatso, fatso at me what they said almost, but not quite, bounced off my fat walls. When my mother walked to her sewing machine and took out of its drawer the belt she kept coiled there and came at me with it, the belt went thud against the fat. The belt didn't cut as hard as it might if I were skinny. But if I were skinny would she have hated me so much? If I hadn't had fat arms like an old lady's maybe my mama would not have beat me so hard, or maybe she would not have beaten me at all. Maybe she would have looked at me and purred, "I love you, darling. I love you."

I looked out my fat-house windows onto the street along which passed thin people, pretty people, popular girls and boys. I was trapped in my fat house. But I was happy in my fat house. I built my house walls with cream gravy and Peter Paul Mounds and Baby Ruth and Mellomints. Inside, my house stayed cold and damp and empty. I had no furnace, no wood stove, no fireplace, no space heater, no clanking radiator. My house was cold.

I squatted down inside my house of fat. Sometimes I said prayers. Sometimes I sang songs. I was a little singer. I wanted to sing my way out of this house of fat. But mostly what I did was wait. I waited for my father, waited to look up into the kindly face that smiled down as the sun did when clouds parted. I waited for my father to take my hand and say, "My little girl. I am taking you away from all this."

Once I arrived at my father's home I had slender legs and slender arms and a flat bony chest. His new wife said, "How cute your little girl is!" We were dancing, he and I. We were kicking up our heels.

This never came true. This was what my mother called "wishing" and when I wished something, she said, "If wishes were horses, then beggars would ride." I hunkered down inside my fat house. I listened to wind shift branches against my fat-house walls. I listened for a voice that would whisper, "I love you." I listened in vain.

I waited for a knock at the door, a ring of a bell, a tap on the window, a shadow on the walkway.

I didn't eat all that much to get myself so fat. Sometimes I even stayed right on the reducing diets and did not cheat and did not steal nickels for Mounds bars and I still didn't lose much weight. All I was was so hungry

Fat Girl

that I would be dizzy and feel like the wind would blow me away or that I would fall down like movie ladies did in a dead faint and need smelling salts. I seemed to be able to inhale, and with each inhalation I expanded like a balloon.

I was filling up on the world. It wouldn't give me anything; I would eat it alive, its air, its trees, its houses, its people. Grammy was right; I was Man Mountain Dean. I would start with my family, then our furniture—the couch, the bed, the dishes, the family photographs in the shoe box—and then I would rub my huge stomach and walk down the sidewalk that led to our now-consumed house and I would start on passersby, would lift them up by the scruff of their jackets and pop them into my mouth like cool pale green seedless grapes.

I hated everyone and yet I wanted everyone to love me. I stood at the playground edge. I watched girls on swings. They had thin legs and pulled their white socks up high on their slender calves. They sailed high, long hair flying behind them. Smiles creased their faces and they opened their eyes wide. I watched boys watch these girls. I knew boys never would watch me this way. I knew they wouldn't chew a grass blade end and narrow their eyes and study my slender legs. I would never have long slender legs. I wanted to be invited to thin girl birthday parties. I wanted to see the cake their mother carried to the party table. The thin girl's mother decorated the thin girl's cake with pink rosebuds heaped one atop another. I could smell from far away the sweet frosting, the strong burning sugar scent.

I loved the boys, even my tormentors. I loved their plaid jackets, zipped up to their scrawny necks, and I loved their home-done haircuts. I loved the salty pork smell these boys gave off when they walked from the windy, cold playground into the steam-heated class-room. I sniffed at them as I sniffed at dinners cooking on the stove.

How could I get them to love me? I was at a loss to figure this. I tried. When girls clutched together near the merry-go-round, I dared myself to stride across the asphalt toward them. I dared myself to make myself a place in the circle they formed. I can still feel the smile form on my full-moon face. I see how I must have looked. I was as sizable as some of their mothers. I weighed more than some of their mothers weighed. I sensed their disgust. I did not want to believe what I felt.

nine

Sometime in third grade I began to try to be funny. I
made fun of a teacher. The boys laughed and some of
the bad girls, they laughed too. I got so I would say anything, just to keep the stage. I became a comic gone
mad, gone wild. I would do anything. I used the few
dirty words I knew. I said "shit" and "piss" and "wiener,"
the word we used for penis. I took the name of the Lord
in vain and I said "Hell," which then was a bad word. I
said "Hell" all the time. I gave the finger. Then one day
a plumber who came to our apartment to fix the toilet
left his Camel cigarettes on the side of the tub. A pack

of matches was tucked inside the cellophane and hid the camel. Mama tossed the cigarettes in the trash and I stole them out. I took them to school. Out on the playground, I walked right up to the boys. I said, "Does anyone want to smoke?" Right away they turned me in to the principal.

It was third grade when another, far worse and truly bad thing happened. It was a snowy Saturday. I know that for sure. Snow sifted down. The sound the snow made was the same sound that sugar made when Grammy, who was visiting, sifted sugar into a cake batter. *Ssss, ssss.*

As I recall, during the years Mama and I lived in New York, my grandmother always came to us in winter. She had moved by this time from her Arkansas farm to a house in Missouri. She made the move, my guess is, because she had become too old to farm. Why she chose this Missouri city, I do not know. Why she came to us in winter, I do not know. Perhaps she had trouble getting around by herself when snow fell and ice slicked her Missouri sidewalk. But come she did.

She was really, really fat by then. I cannot for the life of me recall her seated at the table, eating. Not once. I can only recall her short, stubby body as she stood at various stoves in the various kitchens where she lived and where she came to stay for many months at a time with us. I see her with the butcher knife, chopping cabbages and separating chicken legs from chicken bodies. I see her with a spatula. I see her flip pancakes. I see her lift out a sunny-side-up egg. I see her large muscular

Fat Girl

bare arm. I see her wide face, which as she aged looked more and more like George Washington's.

In New York, Grammy did not wear farm dresses. She wore dark dresses that she closed at the bosom with costume jewelry brooches. She wore diamond studs in her pierced lobes, which, with age, had lengthened, so as she walked the earlobes bobbed. She wore a pink corset. She wore pink underpants, which she called "drawers," whose legs came down to her knees. Varicose veins striated her short fat legs; the veins were navy blue and red. A sour odor rose into the room when she removed her corset and her pink drawers. This odor came close to the sour, yeasty odor that sauerkraut brine takes on.

On this snowy Saturday it was almost time to leave for the movies to go see *The Secret Garden* starring Margaret O'Brien, whom I loved. I told Mama and my grandmother I was going to the movies with Patricia from down the street but that was not true. I was going alone. I had not even asked Patricia if she wanted to go. I knew she wouldn't. Patricia would only frown.

So I got on my sweater and my coat and muffler and my red mittens and got my green shoulder bag purse with my dollar allowance in it, and I went into the kitchen, where my grandmother was peeling Irish potatoes for potato soup, and said good-bye to my grandmother because Mama was in bed with a headache. I said it was time to leave for the movies and my grandmother said to be sure to wear galoshes and wrap up good, which I planned to do anyway because of the snowstorm.

The walk to the movies was ten blocks. It was downhill until Eighth Avenue, where the movie house was. The wind blew hard enough that it blew snow slantwise. I passed the apartment house where a murder had been. I thought about the blood on the sidewalk, that the blood was not bright red, it was dark red, the color of raw liver. It was a family feud, they said, and the family was from Puerto Rico. I remembered the man and his pencil mustache, the kind that scared me. I remembered the two dead people. One was his wife and the other was his wife's brother.

I kept walking downhill past Patricia's apartment house. I wished Patricia liked me but Patricia didn't. Patricia joined up with the boys who sang "I don't want her." Patricia was thin and had good braids and nice dresses but wasn't good at reading and she had buckteeth. People called her "Bugs" after Bugs Bunny and all she did then was stick out her tongue at them and give them the finger. She's who taught me the finger.

I wish I could remember better the movie house interior. I should, because I went there almost every Saturday. I do remember that the seats felt scratchy, like train seats used to feel. I think I remember the lighted red letters over doors on either side of the movie screen: the letters spelled out EXIT. I do remember that the man sat down next to me and that for many minutes while the brightly colored cartoons played I paid no attention to him.

Fat Girl

It was when Margaret got to England that he first touched my arm. I remember that he said something like this to me, "Are you here alone?"

I did not answer. I was not to speak with strangers, especially man strangers. I knew why. The why was the same reason why Grammy told me to stay away from a crazy boy who rode a white horse around her Arkansas farm. The why was my business.

The man wore a red-and-black plaid jacket that years later I realized is called buffalo plaid. He smelled of tobacco. His face, like mine, was fat and round. His hair, like mine, was sandy red and curly. He was thirty to thirty-five.

If there were people behind us, I did not know then and do not remember now. I know that nobody sat on my left side. My navy blue coat and green purse were in the empty seat at my left. He sat on my right side. We were a few seats away from the aisle.

He was eating popcorn. He turned his round moon face to me and smiled and said something like, "Would you care to share my popcorn?" I shook my head no. He insisted. He said, "Please." His voice was deep.

I said, "No, thank you."

We whispered, then, a little bit, back and forth. I do not remember what we said. He probably asked me what grade I was in and I probably told him, "Third." He said his name was Fred and I told him my name, which he said was pretty. He didn't ask personal questions.

Some time passed and he moved his popcorn box to his other hand. He picked up my hand from where it rested on the movie seat's wooden arm. He whispered, "Let me hold your hand."

His hand was warm. I did not know what to do. He leaned down and whispered in my ear that it would not hurt for us to hold hands. He kept my hand folded in his and squeezed it gently.

I did not feel afraid. He ran his finger over my bare wrist, back and forth, back and forth. His doing that felt good. I could hardly keep my mind on the movie screen.

Every time I looked up at him I thought that he and I looked enough alike to be father and daughter. He even had freckles, although they were larger and darker freckles than mine. So while Margaret O'Brien on the screen began to explore the secret garden and to go into the rooms where she was forbidden to go, I began to wonder if Fred was my father. He did have a fat face like my face and he did have a fat belly like my belly. Maybe he had come for me and this offering me popcorn and holding my hand and rubbing my wrist with his thumb was a trick to steal me away from my mother. Maybe Fred really was my father and maybe he thought that if I knew he was my father, I would not go with him. Maybe he thought I hated him the same way my mother hated him. Maybe he knew that my mother said he was lazy and fat and a liar and walked on people like doormats.

Maybe he knew I would be scared of him. I was and I wasn't, no matter who he was. My nose took in tobacco, shaving soap, sweet hair oil and bacon. He smelled like I imagined a father smelled. His face, bathed in the black-and-white movie light, looked kind, very kind.

We talked some more, in whispers. He talked about the snow, that he said he liked snow. He kept rubbing my wrist with his thumb. He said he liked to eat at the Automat and asked me if I liked to eat at the Automat, which I did.

I was bursting to ask him, "Are you my father? Are you?"

I tried to figure out what I would do if he said yes. If he said he was and that he had come to take me away, what would we do when the movie was over? Would we walk fast down to the subway and go to Grand Central and get on the train and ride to his house? I didn't know where his house was, except that it was very far away. I tried to figure out a way to test him, to see if he was my father. Ask him some question, like where I was born, that only my father could answer.

For all my dreamy hopefulness and my violent hunger, I was no dumbbell. I knew that if Fred wasn't my father then all he wanted was to kidnap me. I knew from movies and lurid comic books that if he wasn't my father that as soon as he got me into his car, if he had a car, he would tie a mask over my face so I didn't see where we were going and then he would tie up my arms and legs and put a rag in my mouth so nobody would hear me scream. That was what happened. If the police didn't find you in time, you got cut up in stew-meat-size pieces and there was blood everywhere like there was when the Puerto Rican murdered his wife and her brother.

Fred didn't look to me like a man who cut up little girls. He didn't. But my father's name wasn't Fred and Fred so far hadn't said anything to me like, "I am your father." So while Margaret O'Brien began to make friends with the children at the fancy English estate, I began to allow myself to think about what life would be like if Fred were pretending to be Fred and was really my father. Maybe my father missed me as much as I missed him.

The man who said his name was Fred kept on rubbing his thumb on my wrist. He was humming a tune that I couldn't catch. Then he grabbed my hand and set it atop a hard lump. He squeezed my hand around the hard lump. He moaned, tiny moans, and his lap jiggled, as if there were a jackhammer under his seat. A hot wet gooey substance, like the snot you blew out your nose when you had a bad cold, spurted onto my palm. With my clean hand I snatched my navy blue coat and green purse from the seat and stood up, said, "Excuse me," as I pushed past his knees and ran up the carpeted aisle, past the lights at the end of each aisle, out into the lobby and onto the noisy late Saturday afternoon street. I stood on Eighth Avenue for a moment, to get my bearings. I got into my coat. I slung my green purse over my shoulder. The sky was almost dark. Snow fell hard, at a slant. Cars with lights passed and shoppers, hefting brown Kraft paper shopping bags, hurried along

Fat Girl

through the rapidly falling snow. I began to run, to
thread through the shoppers. While I ran down the slick
sidewalk, past lit storefronts where dressed manne-
quins peered out, past the newsstand, past the man
who sold candied apples, I looked back to see if I saw
the plaid jacket and round moon face.

My heart banged. My breath hurt. I got to the corner, finally, and started the long uphill climb up Forty-
fifth Street to the apartment where my mother had her
headache and my grandmother was making potato
soup. I stopped and looked around and didn't see him.
Men and women, bowed under loads and by wind and
blowing snow, walked up the hill. When I thought nobody was paying attention, I dipped my filthy hand in a
snow bank and cleaned off Fred's mess. I got my red
mittens out and put my hands in them. I ran, then I
walked, then I ran, then I walked, up one lamplit block
after another. I passed the apartment house where the
Puerto Rican killed his family. I passed the apartment
house where Patricia lived. I don't know what, if anything, I said to my mother and grandmother about why
I was home early, or if they noticed I was home early. I
knew I must not tell them what happened and I knew,
too, that even if I had thought I should say what happened that I did not really know *how* to say it.

For a long time after that snowy Saturday I watched
out my bedroom window, down into the street, afraid
that I would see the man in his red plaid coat. When I
walked the six blocks to school, I looked to see if the
man was anywhere near. I was not so much afraid that

he would grab me as I was afraid that he would laugh at me for being such a fool and letting him do that to my hand. I never again went to the movies alone. I made friends with a girl with brown hair and blue eyes whose name was Emily and we started going to the movies together. At the end of that year Grammy went home and Mama and I moved to Manhattan to an apartment near Grant's Tomb.

The story of being a fat child, the story about wanting more than my mother had to give and wanting my father to rescue me might as well have been hammered together with a million nails. But so is what happened that snowy Saturday afternoon at the movies, I realized as I began writing this.

I knew, obviously, that the movie was *The Secret Garden*. So I ordered a copy of the film. I stuck the cassette into my VCR. There, glowing off my television screen, was Margaret O'Brien, so pretty and thin and mean and lost and unhappy. I tried to admire the black-and-white. I like black-and-white films. I like to imagine the colors. I could not watch it. I couldn't. I tried, again and again, to watch the movie, to let myself get baptized by the plot so that I would become a believer in Margaret's dead parents, Margaret's snotty attitude, Margaret's arrival in England. The water wouldn't wash over me. I gave up. I had to.

I had to give up watching *The Secret Garden* because Margaret O'Brien, arriving in England, made the man arrive back in my mind.

ten

**"The child might threaten the
adult she had become."**

—Anita Brookner

The summer before I went to fourth grade, Mama
bought a white bathroom scale and told me to strip
down to my underpants and stand on it. I had not been
naked in front of her for a long time. I had breasts and
did not want her to see them. They weren't real breasts;
they were fat-girl breasts and they sat on top of my
stomach. They perspired underneath and I could lift
them up in my hands like Grammy did when she sprinkled Blue Grass talcum under her dinners.

Mama leaned over the scale to read the numbers. I
weighed 124. Mama was mad. She said she was going

Judith Moore

to put down her foot. I was going to go on a starvation reducing diet and get thin before I started my new school, where I had taken tests to get a scholarship for children who were smart and poor. She said it couldn't go on, my being fat as a goddamn pig. She said she didn't want to take me anywhere. She said she didn't even want to be seen in public with me. She said I would never have friends. She said nobody would want to have anything to do with me. All these things were true. She said I had to lose many pounds, she didn't know how many. I hung my head, shut my fat trap and wisely, said nothing. Nothing was your best bet with Mama.

I sat in our new apartment, which was on the fifth floor and hot, and I sweated and I starved. Lettuce leaves, tomato slices, grapefruit halves, skim milk, dry toast, hamburger patties, skimmed cottage cheese: that was it.

Nights I dreamed candy, baked potatoes with butter melted down in the mashed white interior. I dreamed gravy. I dreamed pot roast slathered with tomato ketchup. Apple pie. I dreamed crumb cake and Chock full o' Nuts whole-wheat doughnuts and candied apples the man in Brooklyn sold and Nathan's hot dogs with relish and mustard. I dreamed creamed spinach and green beans cooked with fatback. I dreamed baked acorn squash with the hole in the middle of its orange flesh filled with pork sausage, the sausage the mince of pig sorrows. Mama when she went to her classes and singing lessons (because she was going to get another master's degree) left nothing in the refrigerator with

113

which I could cheat. But I was determined. I did not want to cheat. When Mama was home and taking a nap, I stayed out of her purse. I did not steal like I had back in Brooklyn so that I could get money for Peter Paul Mounds and Planters peanuts. Truth was, though, that I was so weak and wobbly I could not have gotten down to Broadway to Cirlin's corner grocery if I had wanted to.

I was nuts for the new scale that sat on the black-and-white bathroom tiles. I nearly wore that thing out. All day, while Arthur Godfrey had commercials and while soap operas had commercials, or when I finished another Donald Duck comic book or got a few more pages along in a library book, I pushed myself up out of the easy chair and ran in to weigh myself. I prayed that when I got on the scale more "weight" would be gone. The scale went up and down a pound or two all day and my mood went from joy to despair to joy.

First thing every morning, right after I went to the bathroom, I called for Mama, who rushed in from whatever she was doing. I hopped onto the scale and crossed my fingers hard that I'd lost another pound. Mama read the scale. When I lost a pound, she congratulated me. She said that now that I'd shrunk my stomach it would be easier to lose the weight; she said I wouldn't be as hungry, and I wasn't.

Pretty soon I had lost down to 115. I stood in front of mirrors and pulled in my cheeks and tried to figure what my face would look like skinny. I stood sideways and pulled in my stomach as far as I could pull it. I sat with notebook paper and sheets from Mama's stationery box and drew pictures of pretty dresses that I would wear. I invented scenes in my head where girls called me over to play jump rope. I could jump fast. I dove into Mama's closet and tried to wriggle into her silky grown-up dresses and skirts, but not even her loose dresses fit me. The only thing she owned that fit me were hats. I looked silly in those.

I lost five more pounds, and then no more. I stayed at 110 for many summer weeks. Mama accused me of cheating and I denied I had, and I hadn't. For once, I wasn't lying to Mama, but I had lied for so long that she didn't believe me. She whipped me, I don't know how many times, with the belt. While she whipped me she said I'd better keep my mouth shut or the neighbors would hear. But it truly seemed as if I could get no thinner.

And then, just like that, as summer began to turn to fall, Mama lost interest. I don't know why. Reducing me well may have seemed impossible. But I kept my hopes up and I did not cheat. Every morning I ate my half grapefruit and I ate my Nabisco shredded wheat biscuit poured over with hot skimmed milk. Every lunch I ate my salad and my melba toast and my sliced tomato and cottage cheese. Every night I ate whatever Mama put on my plate and I did not complain.

That summer I got to know the neighborhood. I walked around in the International House Park and admired the equestrian statues. I threw a tennis ball against Grant's Tomb and caught it and threw it again. I strapped on my roller skates and skated down from

Fat Girl

Riverside Drive clear to Broadway several times until the day that I fell and knocked the wind out of myself so bad that I thought I was dead right there on the concrete. I met children my age and played. Mama and I, every Saturday morning, rode downtown on the Fifth Avenue bus so that she could go to her vocal coach's studio, where she sang with her beautiful voice, which was no longer mezzo but had turned pure soprano. She sang Schubert's "Trout Song" and "How Beautiful Are the Feet" from *Messiah* and Mimi from *La Boheme*. While she did this I stayed at the Forty-second Street library to choose my books for the week.

Mama got out her Singer and sewed me dresses. She sewed a navy blue wool jumper and a brown wool jumper and blue-and-white-checked and brown-and-white-checked blouses that went under those jumpers.

When I entered fourth grade, I weighed 106 pounds. I somehow got it in my head that I was thin. I was not thin. I was still fat.

At my new school, a private progressive school in mid-Manhattan, where I was given a full scholarship, life was better than at my old school. Classes were ten or twelve boys and girls rather than the twenty-five in my old school. Because we were closely supervised, I didn't get teased as much. I had quit dropping my *g*'s and speaking in my hillbilly accent. That helped. Two mean boys were in my class and one sweet boy. The sweet one was David, who was kind to everyone. The mean boys were a skinny boy named Pierre, born in France, and Thad. They called me "Pig Face" and sometimes they hissed "Fatso" at me, like so many boys before them.

We went to the gym to tumble. We wore blue bloomers and white shirts and boys wore blue shorts and white shirts. We unrolled the stinky mats. What we were supposed to learn was somersaults, and to do somersaults you put your head down on the mat. Then you rolled slowly onto the back of your neck and flipped yourself. I was so heavy in the butt and stomach that I couldn't turn myself over. I grunted. I sweated myself until I was wet. Everybody in line behind me yelled do it, do it, do it. When boys and girls started laughing, our gym teacher made them apologize. That was more humiliating. That I was so fat I couldn't turn a somersault was embarrassing enough.

Amanda was the other fat girl in our class. Amanda was as big and fat as I was big and fat. She was taller than I was and had larger feet and hands. Probably, now that I think back on Amanda, her face wasn't quite as endearing as mine could be. But her hair—long and blonde and smooth—made up for too widely flanged nostrils and a nose and mouth set too close together. Her father made lots of money. Her mother, when she visited school, from her appearance at least, might not even have been related to Amanda. A tall slender strawberry blonde, Amanda's mother might have been a movie star. She wore furs around her shoulders and pearls on her ears and around her neck and kept her hair in a pageboy and she smelled delicious and her speech was more purr than regular speech. When she came to our schoolroom, she pulled a chair up next to Amanda's and idly stroked Amanda's pretty hair. Every day Amanda brought for her lunch orange carrot sticks, green celery sticks, and sandwiches made with what Amanda said was Cornell bread, designed for helping you lose weight. She brought skimmed milk in a thermos. Amanda's lunch was packed with monogrammed paper napkins and her own straw.

Amanda and I hardly looked at each other and rarely said "Hi." Amanda gazed at me with the same hauteur with which other girls gazed. The only difference between Amanda's regard and that of other girls was that Amanda's eyes showed me no pity. She looked at me with a pure unfettered distaste. I knew better than to engage her with friendliness. I knew better than to take a seat next to her at one of the classroom worktables.

Amanda was dumb. She was so dumb as to be almost slow. When she read aloud she hesitated over simple words. She wrote large, messy numbers on her arithmetic paper. She never raised her hand to answer questions. She was also bossy. She bossed other girls and even boys, and, surprisingly to me, they took it from her. She was always saying, "You can't sit there, Pierre. That's Molly's place." And Pierre would shrug and sit somewhere else. Or she was saying to maybe one of us girls, when we started doodling ballet dancer pictures on our notebook paper instead of doing the capital of Washington State is Olympia, "You'd better do your work or I will tell." She did tell, too.

Our school had a pool in the basement. Was our

class's swimming day Thursday? I think so. I hated swimming day. I hated it when I had to undress down to nothing and then pull on the woolly swimming suits we all wore. The woolly swimming suits were royal blue. They were one-piece and had camisole straps. The straps cut into my shoulders and my dinners pushed out over the low neckline.

When I jumped into the pool the splash was the loudest anyone made. I made bigger splashes than the biggest boys who were fooling around and trying to make big splashes. The coach tried and tried to get me to dive off the diving board. Every time I walked to the end of the board and looked down at the blue-green pool water I knew that if I did this I would die. I was so heavy that my head would go to the bottom and hit the aquamarine tiles and my head would split open and my brains leak out into the water like garbage that floated over by my house on the Hudson River. I would break the diving board. One mean boy said I would. He said, "Old Fatso is going to break the diving board."

These mean boys hurt my feelings. But I agreed with them. They were correct. I *was* fat. What hurt my feelings more was the way girls looked at me, the way that they examined my fat-pocked naked legs and fat naked arms and my round family-way stomach and my sagging dinners. The girls looked at me with such pity in their eyes and such sorrow.

When I walked back from the edge of the diving board I looked at the girls and boys lined up, waiting to take turns. I held up my chin. I looked into the girls' eyes. I thought thoughts that I wanted to send directly into their brains. I thought, "I am sorry I am so fat." I thought, "I am sorry I am scared to dive." I did not dare think, "Be my friend." Or, "Love me as I am." Even today were I to smell chlorine, I would remember that pity in the girls' gazes.

I see myself look back at them with the gaze of someone in grave danger, someone under sentence of death. I felt sentenced. I felt hopeless. I began, that year, to gain back the weight I had starved off over the summer.

Life at home with Mama, believe it or not (which was something I loved to say then, "Believe it or not . . ."), got worse. Mama was extra mean. I was so overweight that I increasingly dreaded the walk up the hill from Broadway to Riverside Drive. I got so out of breath that I began to be afraid I was going to have a heart attack. I know that I was nine and that it was springtime and I was in fifth grade when I began to try to keep from throwing myself out my bedroom window so that I would fall on the concrete and break apart into millions of tiny pieces. I would finally be small.

And yet there's more to this. There is. I have a hard time telling about the two years that we lived in that apartment near Grant's Tomb, a hard time getting my finger on it. Truth was that Mama began to beat me on a regular basis. Beating me began to seem like part of a day's work. She chased me through the small rooms, the brown belt unfurling toward me like an infuriated snake. The belt lived a life of its own, its tip fiery on my bare legs. She screamed, "I am going to cut the blood out of you. I am going to teach you a lesson. I am going to break your will." There were times when the belt drew blood.

Early on I understood this business about breaking my will. Cowboy movies I'd see on Saturday afternoons showed scenes in which cowboys corralled and broke wild horses. The horses reared back their heads and snorted and whinnied. Their unshod hooves stirred dust clouds. The cowboys kept after them, so that no matter how heroic was the horse's resistance, there always came the terrible moment when the cowboy triumphed and the horse relinquished its will.

The shame that Mama's beating me compounded with the shame of my fatness left me cowering. I was nervous. I began to flinch, noticeably, at unexpected noises—backfires in the street, dog barks. If someone bumped me, I jumped.

I'd feel sick to my stomach after a real good beating. I felt shaky and frightened and weak and newly born into an uglier world than it had seemed before the beating started. The word "lurid" describes how I felt the world looked, lurid like bruises. For Mama, the beatings seemed to clear the air, like lightning storms on Midwestern summer afternoons. After the beatings, I felt, well, "beaten." Real beaten.

I had to love someone who beat me. How did I manage this? I did love her and long to please her, but there was no pleasing her. She said that to me, about me, "There's no pleasing you." She said that I was ungrateful, she said, "Give you an inch, you take a mile." She said that I was "never satisfied." She said, "Don't you lie to me, Sister Sue."

I did lie to her. Every single day. I was not satisfied. I did want more.

My mother didn't love me and she did not tell me that she loved me. (I give her credit for that, for not saying, "I love you, darling. I do.") Grammy couldn't stand the ground I walked on and said so. My father forgot me. My mother kept saying that she was nothing but a doormat, that I treated her like my father treated her. "I," she would say, her eyes as wide as a dope addict's eyes, and she metes out this sentence slowly, each word louder than the other, "was nothing but a doormat for your father." By the time she gets to "father," she is howling, and the a in father is a long, long howling a, the vowel of someone who has her leg caught in a trap.

Some time after I was ten and in the fifth grade, I began to make myself invisible to others. I skulked. I said to myself that I was a wallflower and I clung, therefore, to walls. I began more and more to hide myself from myself. I dug down further. I was tired of trying— to get and stay thin, to get along with Mama. Mama and I didn't see much of each other. On weekdays, she rarely arrived home until dinner and she was gone Sunday, because she was the soprano soloist in a midtown church and she frequently sang both morning services and in afternoon chorales and oratorios. Weekday afternoons I practiced piano lessons and played outside, but if Mama was gone, as she sometimes was, in the evenings, or on those Sundays, I felt lonesome and restless. I did not feel frightened. I was more afraid when she was home than when she was not home. When she was home every squeak of a kitchen cabinet door or swish of Kleenex pulled from its box was a scream.

At school, I hadn't liked not being chosen for teams. I hadn't liked not being invited to birthday parties. I hadn't liked it that almost no one wanted to sit next to me at the lunch table. I hadn't liked that I almost always sat alone. But I got so I didn't care that much. I walled myself up, shut myself off. I found ways to amuse myself. I told lies that covered my grief. I said that my father died in the war. I said that my mother was going to be an opera star. I said I got Madame Alexander dolls for Christmas and a three-story dollhouse. I never mentioned Grammy. The lies were flimsy and didn't keep out the cold, but they were better than the truth. The truth was the same truth as always.

I began to chew my fingernails. I turned into a voracious eater whose meal was herself. I ripped and I tore at the flesh around my child nails; I licked, delicately and hungrily, at the blood that popped up in bright droplets at my chubby fingers' ends. I ate myself raw.

My cuticles became infected. My fingers were swollen. When I practiced the scales and arpeggios for piano lessons, when my fingers thumped out the simple

Fat Girl

pieces assigned a child, my fingers hurt. I did not care.
I could not give up this chewing, biting, licking. I could
not give up sucking at my own red blood.

I was not delicious. I was slightly salty. But I was
my own breakfast, lunch, supper and snacks. I was eating myself, I see now, alive.

eleven

"I stand before all humanity recapitulating
my shames . . . and saying: 'I am the lowest
of the low.' Then imperceptibly I pass
from the 'I' to the 'we.' I am like them, to
be sure; we are in the soup together."

—Albert Camus

When you are fat, you are fat every day. But you do not feel fat every day. You look fat, and everyone who looks at you sees a fat girl. And yet you are surprised that everyone sees you as fat. Every time you feel pretty, the spell is broken, either you see yourself in a mirror or some boy screams "Pig Face" or a pretty girl looks at you and then looks away and you see sadness in her eyes or you see disgust and dismay.

Much of the time, almost always when I was alone and occasionally when playing with other children, I forgot my fatness. I forgot how heavily my body weighed

Fat Girl

upon my back, forgot the forty or so pounds of "over-weight" that I carried, jiggling at my hips and riding atop my stomach. "Don't take on airs," Mama often said. That, and, "Don't get on your high horse." So when these hours had passed when I forgot that I was fat, when another child played with me at some "Let's pretend" game and didn't, as was most usual, suggest that I be the mother, for I weighed more than almost everyone's mother, I would be riding that proverbial high horse. "Pride goeth before a fall," Mama said.

The fall always came. Something happened that reminded me that I was obese. Obese was a new word I learned when I was in fourth and fifth grades. "O-bese." That was me.

I had to work extra hard, I felt, to charm and delight in order to make and keep friends. I knew that most children played with me when they had no one else with whom to play. When I went to their apartments for an afternoon their mothers looked upon me with horror. I must have been quite a sight. My fingers, as I mentioned, were bitten bloody; my hips were wider than the hips of many a grown woman, and there was that stomach and those breasts and huge hind end and short, tree-trunk legs.

Also I did not always smell freshly bathed, although I did bathe, every night. I had begun, that year, to sweat heavily, from exertion and anxiety, and the sweat began to smell, an odor like that of Campbell's chicken noodle soup just off the stove. "Pee-yuuu," children said, about my odor. They said, "You stink." They said, "Have you ever heard of soap and water?"

Sweat rings began to form under my blouses' and dresses' arms. I kept my arms stiff at my sides. I could no longer raise my hand in class to answer questions. When I took off my clothes at night my chicken soup odor rose off the cotton and wool. Only my shoes and socks did not stink. I became vain of my feet and polished my stubby toenails with Mama's nail polish.

I have no memory of myself in the bathtub during those years. I do remember that I hated having my long curly hair shampooed because of how much it hurt when Mama brushed out tangles. I screamed at the pain and screamed, too, at the surprise of the pain as the wire dog brush that she used to brush out my curly hair hit tangle after tangle. "Rats," Mama growled at these tangles, "rats."

As if my own smell weren't enough, I had started to notice that the apartment smelled the way women smell. On summer afternoons when Mama lifted her arm, the smell that drifted down mixed the creamy white Odorono deodorant she smeared on her armpits two or three times a day and a wild animal odor, a smell that came out of cages at the Bronx Zoo.

I knew so little of the facts of life that I did not know that everyone eventually got hair under their arms and between their legs. Mama's hair ran down in a line from her belly button to the thatch of hair between her legs. She stood naked in the bathroom and put on her face.

Fat Girl

Mama was pale except for the long ropy nipples at the ends of her dinners and the red hair between her legs that covered up her business. She looked so white she looked sick. After she climbed out of the bathtub, she stood on the bath mat. She put one hand between her legs, under the hair, and with the other hand she shook talcum powder onto herself. Then she set the can down at the edge of the sink and she used both hands to rub the powder into the hair.

The smell I hated most was a meaty odor that drifted out from between my mother's thighs. Oh how Mama and Grammy stunk. That's what I thought, that Mama and her mother, each in a different way, smelled really, really bad. Stink, stank, stunk: not all the Elizabeth Arden Blue Grass talcum and toilet water in the world covered the smell they gave off. Their bodies were engines that produced terrible odors. When Mama had her visitor that was the worst stink. I was more scared of Mama when she smelled that way.

I had no idea why Mama had visitors. When she had them she took pads from the navy blue Kotex box she kept in the bathroom and she put those pads between her legs. She got blood on the pads. She lay in bed and called to me to bring wet cold washrags to put on her forehead. She spread out a bath towel across the bottom sheet when she had her visitor. She always put her behind right on that towel, then. When I asked why Mama did this, she said it was to keep the visitor from getting on the sheets and staining them, because even with Clorox you couldn't get out the visitor.

Judith Moore

"You will get your visitor someday," Grammy said when I was nine going on ten. She said it in her usual hateful way, scowling at me. And then Mama, who was sitting at the table and looking more pale than usual, her countenance drained of color, said, real mean, to her mother, "Don't talk to her about that. She already knows too much for her years." Then Grammy told her not to take that tone with her and then my mother started crying and I said excuse me, that I had to go to the bathroom, and I left.

I didn't want any visitor. I did not want to have to spread out a towel in the bed so I wouldn't get visitor on the sheets and I did not want to smell the way Mama smelled and I did not want all that hair to grow all over me and creep up into my belly button. I pulled one of the white pads out of the Kotex box and I took down my pants and put the white pad between my legs and held it tight against my business. I hated the way it felt and I stuffed it back into the box.

Mama was worse to me when Grammy was there. The two of them were always sitting at the kitchen table and drinking Folgers coffee and when I popped up and asked what they were talking about, Mama or Grammy said, "Little pots have big ears." They said shut your trap, which was not fun, to be told all the time Shut up Shut up. They set each other off, Mama and Grammy, and Grammy would criticize the way Mama wore her skirts tight (which she did) or she would complain that Mama wouldn't take her to some Broadway show and Mama would clatter from the room on her high heels and sit in the bathroom and sob. Mama did lots of crying when her vile mother was there and I felt sorry for her. They were poisonous snakes, those two, and you couldn't be too careful. With them, you never knew what might set them off.

I hated them and I needed them and I prayed to God and Jesus to help me love them. I was nobody's fool. I had no place to go. From what I read about orphanages, I did not want to go to one.

I was rarely unhappy when I was alone in my room, the door closed between Mama and me. I was happy for hours at a time at school, for I was a superb student, able at every subject, and particularly able at any subject that demanded reading and comprehension and retention of what I read. If I didn't know it, I wanted to know it. Ignorance was bliss.

When we moved to Manhattan, I had started going to Sunday school and church. I loved to sit in church directly beneath the stained-glass window where, in the colored glass, Jesus sat on a chair and suffered the little children to come unto Him. I said prayers. I said "Now I lay me down to sleep." I said the Lord's Prayer. Even though Mama didn't believe that anything happened after you died except that you rotted, I began to want to believe that God and Jesus cared about me. If I took seriously what preachers in church and teachers in Sunday school said about who God and Jesus were, then it seemed possible that I could be wrapped in their love. I understood God, in part, as the ultimate equal opportunity love provider. I understood church members and church workers as God's employees. I hoped that if I prayed I could become a good girl and not do what I did that made Mama chase me with the belt and knock me one across the face so hard that my cheeks rattled. I prayed silently over my food, because Mama wouldn't tolerate any praying at the table. I prayed to get thin. I prayed not to play with myself. I prayed to make friends.

I made friends with a woman who lived two floors above us and had sung in a choir with my mother. Her name was June and I was permitted to call her June, an honor in those days when relations between children and adults were somewhat formal. She was tall and heavyset and had natural ash-blonde hair. Her parents were Norwegian and June had large features and blue eyes that I thought of as Norwegian eyes. My mother wasn't crazy about June, whom she described as "horse-faced" and "man-crazy" and "broad in the beam." June was nice to me, very nice. She often took short trips out of town to perform or to attend master classes or to visit family, and when she made these trips she paid me twenty cents per day to take care of her mail.

The mailboxes were on the first floor. Each mailbox had its own combination. My job was to look in her box and see if she had mail. If I did see letters I spun the combination and slipped out her envelopes and magazines (every week she got *Life* and *Look* and she also subscribed to *Etude* and *Harper's Bazaar* and *Vogue*

Fat Girl

and *Theater Arts*). I had a cardboard box that I kept in my bedroom where I stored June's mail. On her arrival home, she handed me a wrapped and beribboned gift. These gifts were items my cash-strapped mother would not have given me—a purple leather purse, children's cologne, a multicolored lollipop the size of a dinner plate, Nancy Drew mysteries, a gold locket, a charm bracelet from which hung silver ballerinas, a wooden flute, and an amazing zither on whose strings I plucked out "Sentimental Journey" and "Blue Skies."

She took me out one Saturday to a soda fountain and she ordered fizzy chocolate sodas and she asked if I wanted to be a pianist or a violinist when I grew up and I said I didn't want to be either, that I was sick of the piano and that the violin, on which I recently had begun lessons, was too hard. I showed her where the strings had raised calluses on the fingers of my left hand. Other times she took me for hamburger lunches at a drugstore lunch counter. She told me about when she was a girl in upstate New York and how she and her two sisters ice-skated on a pond behind their house and how their mother dressed the trio for family parties and church in matching dresses. I asked if she could skate figure eights and she said she could, plus, when she was young, she could twirl and twirl and twirl on the metal toe of one skate blade.

June was nice to me. Her hands on my bare arm or my cheek were cool and dry and she smelled spicy from the perfume that she dotted behind her large ears. I'd guess that not a week passed after she and I first met before I began to talk with her in my mind and to tell her what happened at school and at my violin or piano lesson. I began to ride the elevator two floors past our floor to June's floor. I'd step off the elevator and stand outside her door and press my ear against her door and listen. Sometimes she would be playing Bach Two-Part Inventions or Chopin Preludes on the Acrosonic spinet in her living room; other times she would be vocalizing, her mezzo running up and down the scales, or she would be trying out a Schubert song, her voice then exploratory, returning again and again to the same phrases. Not infrequently I heard her talk on the telephone.

Sometimes, too, when June wasn't home from one of the classes she attended or the choir practices or church services or voice lessons, I might strap on my roller skates and skate in front or our apartment house or I might sit on the long wooden bench near the mailboxes and read. If June arrived while I skated or while I turned pages in my book, I acted surprised. I acted as if I'd happened to be there, where she was. If a day passed or two days and I didn't see June, I felt broken and in need of mending. And, if, as occasionally happened, June was distracted and didn't pay me much mind, if she was walking with someone and said "Hi" and didn't stop to talk, I felt panic stricken. I feared it was over between June and me.

The year that I was ten and in fifth grade June went on sabbatical to Germany for spring semester. She paid me to water her African violets. The violets sat in small pots and each pot sat in a saucer. I was, June told me, "to water from below." No way was I to get water on the violets' fuzzy leaves. If water got on those leaves, then brown spots would form on the leaves. Her hand on my neck was cool as we stood at mid-morning in the bright eastern exposure in which the violets flourished. I didn't care one way or another about houseplants. But because June spoke so passionately about these flowering wonders, I conceived a mild fondness for them. I promised I'd love them as if they were my own. I meant what I said.

June hadn't been gone more than a few days before I began coming home after school and hanging out in her apartment. I rode the two flights to her apartment. I unlocked her door. I made myself at home. I made believe she was my mother or a sister who adopted me when our parents died. I made believe she would be home any minute. I threw myself in her chintz-covered easy chair with its wide and comfortable arms. If I'd known to say it, I'd have said, "What bliss."

Bit by bit I rifled everything she owned. I examined her huge brassieres, whose cups easily would have held cantaloupes. I examined her navy blue Kotex box and the Kotex pads. I tried on her costume jewelry necklaces and her high-heeled shoes. I sat in her bedroom pale green velvet slipper chair and practiced dangling the high-heeled shoe off my toe the way that ladies in movies dangled shoes. I admired her Christmas and birthday cards and Valentine cards and the many sympathy cards sent her when her father died. I read letters from her mother and her sisters. These letters were mostly the boring, "How are you? I am fine" letters. Some, though, written by June's mother and sisters, were about her father's long death from stomach cancer. And yet other letters, letters two and three years old, referred to a boyfriend who had married another woman. They had a child, a son, and were living in Boston. June, her mother wrote, "was better off without him." This new knowledge about June made me feel as if she and I, unlucky as we were in love, had something deep in common. I thought then that I had heard sadness in her singing and seen sadness in her blue eyes and I loved her more.

I went through June's pantry. June had B&M baked beans. I opened the can and I spooned the beans, cold from the can, into my mouth. The beans tasted vivid and rich and sweet in a way that the same beans, eaten warm at the kitchen table in our apartment, never tasted. You can guess the rest. I heated and slurped up June's Campbell's soups, her chicken gumbo, pepper pot, chicken noodle, beef noodle, and nasty cream of celery. I right away ate her saltines and left the empty box. How did I even begin to imagine that the crackers would replenish themselves? I ate her canned cling peaches and albino white pear halves and gaudy fruit cocktail; I ate her golden raisins and dark sultana raisins and dried Calmyra figs and I stuffed into my mouth lumps of her brown sugar.

I sat at June's kitchen table, my elbows up on its pretty oilcloth cover. I wiped my mouth with the paper napkins from her napkin holder. I imagined that June talked to me, in that soothing mezzo, about her pink and white and purple-flowered violets and their care. She told me about her father, and how he taught her and her sisters to twirl on ice. With one of her sheer cotton hankies she patted at the corners of her eyes and told me about the boyfriend, how handsome he was, how she loved him.

When the solid food began to run out I made tea with June's Lipton tea bags, even though I didn't like tea. I enjoyed drinking the tepid Lipton's from June's translucent china cups. Months passed and June's shelves emptied.

I had not permitted myself to notice that the shelves, well stocked when June left, were almost bare. I re-arranged boxes and cans that remained—unsweetened pie cherries, Chock full o' Nuts coffee, grapefruit sections, green turtle soup, pink salmon—so that these cans stood at the front of the shelves. I didn't recognize how dirty and food-spotted June's apartment had become. Even though I tried hard to be tidy, her apartment, spotlessly clean when she left for Europe, by summer was filthy. I had dropped cracker crumbs and dribbled soups and canned fruit juices and heaven knows what on her carpets and her upholstery.

I ran the carpet sweeper. I scrubbed with a washcloth at the stain on the chintz that covered her armchair and my scrubbing enlarged the area of filth. As I looked at that wet, filthy spot on the arm of the chair, a spot that darkened a pale pink rose and pastel green leaves, it was as if I had awakened from a long pleasant dream through whose warm tropic landscapes I weightlessly floated.

I was in trouble. I took for granted that when June returned she'd tell my mother I'd eaten her food and made a mess. I felt sick to my stomach. The day that she was to return, a day to which earlier I had so looked forward, was now a day I dreaded. I was so frightened about what would happen—hearing my mother scream that I was a thief, watching my mother get out the belt and scream that she'd beat me, the first sharp strike and sting when the leather belt's metal tip slapped against my bare leg.

The worst part was not my fear of the beatings. I was accustomed to beatings. What I was not accustomed to was what I felt for June. I loved her and I felt guilty and ashamed. I had let her down. I had stolen from someone who loved or, at least, liked me, someone who trusted me.

June returned. I walked into our apartment building and she was in the lobby, suitcases stacked around her. She ran toward me, teetering on her high heels. She hugged me against her huge breasts and she kissed me on my cheeks. My school was out and it wasn't time for me to leave for camp. I waited in my apartment for the phone call from June to my mother or for June's knock on our door.

Several days passed and June called to say hello to

my mother and came by to bring us gifts from Germany and to give me an envelope into which she'd slipped two ten-dollar bills. She praised me for the excellent care she said I had given her African violets. The few times we ran into one another in the lobby or out on the side-walk, she enfolded me in her warm hug.

twelve

"Even before a model, you draw from
memory. The model is a reminder. Not of a
stereotype that you know by heart. Not even
of anything you can consciously remember."

—John Berger,
A Painter of Our Time

Two days after fifth grade ended Grammy's neighbor in
Missouri called to say that Grammy had had a stroke.
Uncle Carl was on his way from Oklahoma to Grammy's
house in Missouri. Mama packed us up and got us to
Grand Central and on the train. Grammy was bad off
when we arrived. Mama and Uncle Carl decided that
because he had his summer teaching job the best thing
was for Mama to stay with Grammy and for me to go
stay with Carl in his three-bedroom house near the college. Uncle Carl and I drove to his house in his pea-green

Fat Girl

Chrysler New Yorker, which was his pride and joy. He drove, people said, like a bat out of hell.

This town where Uncle Carl had his house was the town where Mama grew up and where my father had been born and raised. Uncle Carl's house was on one side of the college and the house where I lived with my parents and the houses where my father and mother grew up were on the other side of the college. I thought it was strange to be in a town where my father's parents and uncles and aunts and half sister and half brother and whole brother lived and not to see them. I was trying to figure how I could see their houses. I did not think I wanted to meet them because they were the enemy. Why I felt that way is the awful things my mother and my grandmother said about my father and his family. Uncle Carl kept his mouth shut on the subject.

So there I was, ten going on eleven, at Uncle Carl's house in my own bedroom with blue walls and double bed with a blue bedspread. I was happy. Now I understand that at that age I hardly knew what happiness was. This feeling I felt—happiness—was a feeling I hardly could identify, but living with Uncle Carl was happiness to me.

Almost the minute we got to his house and opened our suitcases, Uncle Carl said the cupboard was bare and for me to get into the car and off we would go to Piggly Wiggly. "Get what you want, Toots." I couldn't believe he meant this.

Uncle Carl didn't do squat when I started piling into the cart everything I liked to eat and some things I

wanted to eat and never had tasted—cherry ice cream,
for instance, and a TV dinner with a picture of a fried
chicken leg on the box. I heaped in Grapette and Royal
Crown Cola and Nehi orange and sacks of Planters
peanuts with Mr. Peanut printed on the see-through
sack. I was a Mr. Peanut fan and liked to watch him
dance on his sign in Times Square.

There are unhappy times, though, in this story, and
unhappy I knew about. Like when my mother called
from Grammy's house when Grammy still was in the
hospital and Mama was sitting with her day and night.
My uncle loved his wretched old mother and when
Mama described how the old gal was wasting away and
said that the stroke was only the half of it, that she had
a cancer that was eating her vital organs, tears ran
down Carl's handsome face and he rubbed tears off
himself with a handkerchief. After Uncle Carl said,
"Good-bye, Kathleen," he sat hunched with his head in
his hands. Then he pulled himself off the telephone
bench and strode into the bathroom and closed the
door and turned on water. He stayed there a while.
When he walked back out, he was smiling.

One incredibly hot morning after I'd been there a
month and Grammy had been moved home to her
house and my mother was nursing her, Uncle Carl was
hunkered over his four-burner gas stove. The ther-
mometer nailed to the scrawny poplar tree outside, were
anyone to read it, would have read 100 degrees. And it
was only early morning, a summer Saturday morning in
central Oklahoma. Uncle Carl wore red plaid shorts.

Fat Girl

Wrapped around Uncle Carl's head was a cotton tea towel. The tea towel featured a smiling Aunt Jemima in repeat print. Thus, many many Aunt Jemimas wreathed Uncle Carl's head, and sweat soaked all of them.

What it appeared Uncle Carl was doing, standing by his gas stove, was cooking. In one hand he held a yellow yardstick. He stuck the yellow yardstick into the canning kettle and stirred and stirred and looked perturbed. The water bubbled in the kettle.

I was sitting at the kitchen table. I was still young enough and short enough that my feet didn't think of touching the floor. You could talk away to Uncle Carl without getting in trouble and you could ask anything. I asked how it was going. I probably wiped with the back of my wrist the milk mustache that dried above my upper lip. I probably thought how great it is that my mother wasn't there and that nobody was going to snap at me about using my napkin. I didn't even have a napkin.

Uncle Carl stirred with his yellow yardstick. He said that he hoped this little experiment worked. He said that his friend Jon was coming that afternoon (which I knew) from Tulsa to help Uncle Carl redecorate and he said he wanted to get this bedspread dyed chartreuse and on the clothesline and dry before Jon got there. Everything in his bedroom was going to be chartreuse. He and Jon had already painted the walls chartreuse.

Jon was an interior decorator. He was bringing from Tulsa fabric for the drapes. They were going to hang the drapes and that night they were going to give a dinner

Judith Moore

party that Uncle Carl called "The Chartreuse Gala." Everybody was coming: Max, Len, Dan (Mr. Huffman to me), Alfred, Knox, Terry, Boris, Bob. All the food except for T-bones was going to be green and even the T-bones would have green basil butter. Jon was bringing the basil from Tulsa. They had everything in Tulsa, and when people in Oklahoma talked about Tulsa you would have thought it was New York City.

What was in Uncle Carl's kettle wasn't dinner, it was his white chenille bedspread. Uncle Carl had used four boxes of Rit Dye, one green and three yellow, and he was telling me that he hoped to God, whom, by the way, he did not believe in, that green and yellow make chartreuse. One reason Uncle Carl was sure there was no God was that nobody who created the world in seven days would ever create that depressing First Methodist Church where Uncle Carl played the organ. If he didn't need money, he was always saying, you wouldn't catch him dead in that church. As it was, he sat on a folding chair by the organ and dozed through sermons.

But Uncle Carl was not talking about God or money or his full-time job teaching organ and eighteenth-century counterpoint at the Agricultural & Mechanical College. He was wiping sweat with the Aunt Jemima towel and he was saying it's hotter than Hades and I was agreeing, because my shortie nightie was damp from sweat on the panties part and even though I was usually hungry, I was not hungry. I was so hot. Uncle Carl, who saw that I was dawdling with my Cheerios, said, "Maybe, Toots, we should have root beer floats."

143

Fat Girl

Which was something I loved about Uncle Carl, that you didn't have to eat the right food and he never said the word "diet" to you or "fat." He never fed me hard-boiled eggs and melba toast. Another thing I loved was that he never yelled at me except to say "Watch out" when I was about to step on a bee, and he never slapped me or kicked my fat hind end and he was incredibly gentle when, every morning, and many evenings, he braided my long auburn hair into two pigtails. He didn't brush my scalp and he didn't yank when he braided. Also, he did a pretty good job of braiding. He didn't say that I had to practice the piano, which was a relief, because I was sick of the piano. During the day while Uncle Carl taught organ students and classes, he dropped me off at the pool or the library and sometimes at movies.

I had also made a friend. The head minister at the Methodist church, Poe Williams, had a daughter my age named Glenda. Reverend Williams had a birthmark that stained one side of his face. The birthmark was purple and the purple skin was corrugated. Anyway, one day he suggested in his sonorous preacher voice to Uncle Carl that maybe Glenda and I could go swimming together. I already knew Glenda because she was in my Sunday school class where Uncle Carl left me off while he rehearsed the choir before the church service. Glenda was a thin, beautiful blonde. She wore lipstick and already had real breasts and her period.

I have a snapshot of Glenda and me that Uncle Carl

took. We are holding our rolled-up towels, inside of which are our wet bathing suits, and we are walking out of the pool house door. Glenda is smiling at the camera, a smile that shows all her white teeth. She has tied a bandana over her hair, and she is wearing white shorts and a skimpy halter top and flip-flops. She looks chic. She looks like a movie star. My face is so fat you can almost not see my eyes and I am wide, wide, wide across the hips and chest, and my shirt pulls at the buttons where I was growing even fatter on Uncle Carl's treats and the delicious lunches Uncle Carl and I ate, on discount, at the college student union.

Next to this sylph of a poised and smiling blonde, I look particularly heavy and slow. I am surprised that Glenda, who already had been elected cheerleader, would appear in public with me. She did. She introduced me to everyone she knew at the pool. I thought at first that naturally she would desert me for her pretty and popular friends, yet she never did. If she is still alive out there somewhere, I hope she is happy. She deserves happiness for being so kind to me.

I also spent afternoons in the student union, where Uncle Carl and I ate lunch almost every weekday. I ate out more that summer than I ever ate out again in my entire life. The student union cafeteria offered mashed potatoes and gravy and meat and vegetables and pies and cakes and salads (over which I poured Thousand Island dressing), and all Uncle Carl said was, "Get what you want, Toots." I ate and ate and ate and I was never

Fat Girl

hungry. Uncle Carl gave me quarters and fifty-cent pieces for candy bars and sodas that I could buy and eat while he was teaching.

That summer morning, while Uncle Carl boiled his bedspread, he let me put down my Cheerios for his obese yellow tomcat, Tom, at whom Uncle Carl often yelled because Tom got into the urn where Uncle Carl grew an avocado tree and did what Uncle Carl called his "toilet," which was shitting. While the yellow-green water bubbled, Uncle Carl and I sat at the table and sipped cold root beer and spooned out the cold vanilla ice cream with long iced tea spoons from the fizzy brown root beer froth. Uncle Carl said "Mmmm" and licked his ice cream lips. He sighed, "A busy busy day ahead!" His eyes were huge and brown. "Bedroom eyes," my mother said they were. He had long thick lashes like horses have and he opened his eyes wide when he looked at you. He said we were going to clean house, we were going to get this bedspread on the line whether it turned chartreuse or not, and he was going to Piggly Wiggly. He unwrapped his sopped Aunt Jemima rag from his head and started writing on his lined pad: T-bone steaks, garlic, lettuce, Spanish onions, toma- toes, butter, celery, green bell peppers, Idaho potatoes, grapefruit, vanilla ice cream, and many limes, because Jon, he said, and he smiled when he said it, was going to make daiquiris. We had liquor because even though Oklahoma was a dry state, everybody bought liquor from a bootlegger and you bought lots of liquor at once.

Judith Moore

Uncle Carl had a closet of liquor. Uncle Carl's sweat fell
on his list and smeared his writing and he said, "Hell's
bells." Then he calmed down and said that we had so
much to do before Jon showed up from Tulsa, and that
after we got the housework done he would drop me at
the swimming pool, which was six blocks from his
house.

First, Uncle Carl had to get the bedspread on the
line and he told me to hold wide open the screen door
that led from the kitchen to the backyard, and I hopped
up and unstuck my sweaty self from the chair and did
that, and flies swooped in past me and poor Uncle Carl
grunted as he carried the heavy, steaming pot out to the
grass. Uncle Carl scalded his hands trying to wring out
the spread and he got chartreuse water on his feet and
hands and legs and he was screaming, and worst of all
green spots splotched the spread, and Uncle Carl said
"Hell's goddamn bells" and turned the garden hose on
himself to cool off. He finally got the spread hitched on
the clothesline and wrung it more and then laughed his
deep laugh.

I won't go into how we cleaned house like banshees
for two hours or how Uncle Carl kept going to stare
through the screen door at his ruined bedspread, which
decades before tie-dye looked tie-dyed, and how he
scrubbed green spots off the stove and how we got ourselves dressed and Uncle Carl let me off at the pool after
saying thank you, Toots, for the help. I won't bore you
with how I changed into my suit, which had a flowered

Fat Girl

skirt, and how I floated on my back. I was buoyant and floated easily in among every other floating and splashing body and I looked up into the blue blue cloudless sky and thought my almost-eleven-year-old's thoughts. I didn't think as much about my fat. I thought about what was going to happen next in my life.

At Uncle Carl's house I felt guilty because I was so happy with him that I didn't stop to care that my grandmother was suffering. One among many things I liked about living with Uncle Carl was that when we went shopping or when he left me at the pool or the library or when we went out to dinner with his friends, we looked like father and daughter. I imagined that people thought, when they looked at Carl, holding my hand and chatting with me, "That's his little girl." I felt proud to be alive with him. He looked spiffy in his summer seersucker suits and starched shirts and bow ties and proper panama summer hat (men still wore hats then). I was enchanted with the idea that to all the world I appeared to be a girl with a father who loved her.

I liked that Uncle Carl's house smelled mannish. I couldn't get enough of his aftershave that he slapped onto his cheeks after he shaved or his soap that he kept in the shower stall. Nothing smelled of that between-the-legs odor that my mother gave off and Grammy, too. Also at Uncle Carl's house I got many compliments from him and from his friends, who were both men and women, that I didn't think how fat I was and ugly and awkward and unlovable. Even at the swimming pool I did not feel fat, although I was stuffed tight into my

Judith Moore

flowered bathing suit, which was expansive enough for three Charleston Grey watermelons. When boys at the pool called me Fatso I hardly cared. I gave the finger, which was a very New York thing to do, and that shut them up.

Another happy part of what was happening in my life was that I had a heart-stopping crush on Poe Williams's assistant pastor, Raymond Fisher. I thought about Reverend Fisher a lot. What I felt for him was part schoolgirl ardor and part longing for a father. I'd felt this way before about movie stars and teachers at my school and about my violin teacher, who was handsome and kind and had a wealthy brunette girlfriend and a fancy aqua convertible. I had photos of Montgomery Clift and James Dean, Robert Mitchum (my heartthrob since second grade), Marlon Brando. I cut out these photos from *Life*. I put the photos in my wallet in the plastic sleeves meant for friends and family.

Reverend Fisher wasn't handsome. He looked like Billy Graham—the dirty blond hair and wide expressive face, the bright blue hungry Confederate soldier eyes. Even at that age, I knew Reverend Fisher wasn't all that smart. What he was was emotional. I loved emotional. Reverend Fisher preached the Sunday night youth service that we had after MYF—Methodist Youth Fellowship. Glenda got me going to this. She and I weren't quite old enough for it, but they let sixth-graders join. After the MYF meeting we gathered in the sanctuary and sang hymns and then Reverend Fisher climbed up in the pulpit. At night, we didn't wear Sunday best. The boys wore slacks and a shirt and the girls wore cotton circle skirts and blouses. The girls cinched the skirts with wide elastic belts. I didn't have anything that grown-up and wore plaid school dresses. The sleeves had gotten so tight on the dresses that Uncle Carl cut them underneath where you couldn't see the cut.

At this night service that summer, the sanctuary was hot. The ceiling fans turned and turned. Moths flew in through open windows. My bottom sweat onto my skirt and my skirt stuck to the wood pew. That's how hot it was even at seven-thirty in the evening in Oklahoma in July. The preachers didn't wear robes; they wore suits. Reverend Fisher wore a blue suit that was tight on his beefy body. When he preached he leaned over the pulpit and searched out the rows of our upturned eyes. He wrung his hands. He waited for us to be quiet. Only then did he speak his first words.

He spoke in hushed tones. The only reason we could hear him was that a microphone was rigged up on the pulpit. Out in the congregation you could hear us young people breathe. We were one starving animal, waiting for our master to feed us. He let out his sentences slowly. He let his thoughts uncoil. He opened his hands, palms up, and his hands offered infinite tenderness, a tenderness that I desired. He said, "Jesus suffered." He said in a moaning way that made me feel close to him, "Jesus suffered because he loves you. Because the Father loves you."

The service ended with an altar call. Reverend

Judith Moore

Fisher urged us to come to the altar and confess our sins and give our lives to Jesus and be blessed. I wanted to be blessed. I was a dirty girl and I knew it. I played with myself, I told lies, I stole dimes and quarters and an occasional Liberty half-dollar from my mother's purses, although I had never stolen anything from Uncle Carl. I stole food from June. I read her mail. I took the Lord's name in vain. I thought the stray dirty thought and recently I had been reading Uncle Carl's *Sexology* magazines, which had stories about how animals and fish had sex. There was an article that was my favorite called "The Sex Life of Sea Horses."

I tried hard not to do these things and I knew I did not try hard enough. I'd end up in a girls' reformatory. I'd get sent to the electric chair. I feared hell's flames. I feared being stretched on a rack and tortured and tormented in hell by vicious fun-loving devils and I also was mildly turned on by hell's images. Except for the fire. The fire did not turn me on. Heaven, however, seemed such a beneficent milky spot where all the time quiet music played. I imagined clouds and God the Father sitting up straight on His golden throne and Jesus His Son who suffered me to come unto Him.

While Reverend Fisher stood by the altar rail, we sang:

> Softly and tenderly Jesus is calling,
> Calling for you and for me;
> See, on the portals he's waiting and watching,
> Watching for you and for me.

Fat Girl

And then we sang:

> **Jesus calls us; o'er the tumult**
> **of our life's wild, restless sea,**
> **day by day his clear voice soundeth,**
> **saying, "Christian, follow me."**

Reverend Fisher slipped out of his sweat-soaked blue jacket and draped the jacket over the altar rail. He stretched out his arms and turned his hands, pink palms up. You could see the huge sweat rings on his white shirt and sweat spots on the chest of his shirt. Sweat ran down his face. His blue eyes pleaded with us. While we crooned Jesus is calling, Reverend Fisher's eyes looked down into us, past our breasts to where our hearts hung on veins and arteries, beating and beating. Our hearts hung in our chests like swallows' nests hung off trees. He saw into our hearts, Reverend Fisher did, and what he could not see didn't matter, because God knew. His eye was on the sparrow and I knew He watched me.

I wanted to feel my hard heart soften and break open. I wanted to love my mother. I wanted to love Grammy, who was suffering torments. I gripped the Methodist hymnal, filled with its Wesley hymns, and tried to give myself over and couldn't. I tried to feel sorrow for my sins and all I felt was fear.

I was afraid of myself. I was afraid of the evil in me that seemed to rise out of nowhere and take me over.

thirteen

"When you realize you are lost,
the mind is instantly animated with a kind
of stoic cheerfulness. How much worse
could it be, you think."

—John Cheever,
Journals

So while I floated in the pool on my back and looked up into the sky and puffy clouds I thought about heaven and Reverend Fisher. I wanted him to pay attention to me, but he showed no interest in me. Maybe Jesus knew everybody's name but I didn't think Reverend Fisher knew mine. His wife taught Glenda's and my Sunday school class. She was a career woman who worked as secretary for the American Cancer Society. She was pretty and kind and wore high heels and dresses with lace collars. She was blonde, like her husband, and had her hair in a permanent, and she wore a perfume that smelled of roses. Reverend and Mrs. Fisher had two sons, both younger than I was. I felt jealous of the sons for getting to live with people who were as sweet as their mom and dad were.

Even before it was three o'clock that Saturday, when I was supposed to start home from the pool, my skin had withered and I was lonesome because Glenda wasn't there and neither were her friends that I knew well enough to say hello to. I got out of my suit and slipped on my shirt and my white shorts and walked home fast and hurried in the back door determined to drink Grapette and eat a sack of Mr. Peanut.

Nobody was in the kitchen and I didn't hear a sound except fans whirring. Lettuce was heaped up on the cutting board and so were garlic cloves mashed into a mushy heap and already-baked potatoes for the twice-baked potatoes and chopped parsley and lime halves. I smelled lime juice and garlic. I smelled baked potato. I was nuts for Uncle Carl's twice-baked potatoes, which were as good as restaurant food.

Then I heard a cat sound. Up on the counter was fat Tom. He'd torn off the white butcher paper and was ripping at raw T-bone. I tried to snatch him off the T-bones. He scratched me. He hissed. I grabbed the broom. I swatted him. With steak in his mouth he jumped off the counter and streaked out through the kitchen screen door, which I hadn't shut.

I was worried about the steak. I hurried through the dining room, where the table was set with china and wineglasses. I walked into the hall and saw into Uncle

Judith Moore

Carl's bedroom, and he and Jon were stretched across the chartreuse bedspread and they were naked except for boxer shorts, and they were kissing and didn't see me or hear me. By the bed on the chartreuse scatter rug, I saw four empty Grapette bottles and I knew, then, there wouldn't be Grapette for me.

I didn't know what to think about the kissing, I really didn't. I didn't mind. And, in fact, I lied just now. They actually were naked and I put them into boxer shorts so that you wouldn't be shocked or disgusted. But I truly didn't mind. I'd seen butts before. I'd seen kissing.

What I hadn't seen was a cat eating T-bone. I went back to the kitchen and started screaming, "Uncle Carl, Uncle Carl, come quick," and next thing Jon and Uncle Carl were there, dressed in shirts and seersucker slacks, which was what men wore then in summer, and I was telling how I got home and was thirsty and went to get Grapette and Tom was on the counter tearing at T-bone. I showed where he scratched me, which was bleeding, and told the truth about how I left the screen door open, and Tom streaked out with steak in his mouth. Jon, who was as old as Uncle Carl was then, which was fifty-something, shook his head and looked sad. Jon had a long, narrow head and skin that always looked tanned because he used a sun lamp. Uncle Carl laughed and Jon shrugged and said, "Que sera, sera," and that company would be here at five and we'd better rub garlic onto the steaks and into the wooden salad bowl.

Uncle Carl rustled in the refrigerator and got out

155

what he said was the last Grapette and I drank it down. He and Jon tied on aprons and Jon went to the living room and plopped on the record player his Edith Piaf 78 that he'd brought from Tulsa. It was Edith Piaf singing "La Vie En Rose." I said I hated garlic smell and Uncle Carl said, "Well, then, Toots, why don't you cut the grapefruits in half for me and tip out the seeds?" I knew how to do that and I did. I would have done just about anything for anyone who called me "Toots," especially Uncle Carl.

I stood by the counter and cut grapefruits in half and tipped out seeds until I felt like a grapefruit factory worker. I didn't say a word about the cat hair on the counter, which would have made my mother go mad. I didn't ask if they knew where Tom was with that T-bone because I could tell that they didn't care. While Uncle Carl carried on with his garlic smearing onto steaks and French bread and the salad bowl, Jon cut limes and squeezed juice and sang with Edith Piaf, and the singing made Uncle Carl wince because Jon was off-pitch. They talked about their menu and in what order to do things. They listed the menu aloud—the crackers with cream cheese and chives, the Green Goddess dressing for the green salad, the green beans, the Chartreuse to pour over the ice cream, and so on and so on.

Jon had already scooped out the baked potatoes and mashed the potato with parsley and butter and put mashed-up potato back in the skins. Once I got the grapefruit done, Uncle Carl asked me to line up the halves on the cookie sheet, which I did, and he opened

the crème de menthe bottle and poured green liqueur
onto the grapefruit halves until the fruit turned green
for the chartreuse evening. Uncle Carl told me they were
going to broil the grapefruit and serve them for appetiz-
ers. Jon, in the middle of "La Vie En Rose," said to no
one in particular that people were going to love the
grapefruit. I didn't say I wasn't so sure.

Uncle Carl asked if I'd seen the drapes and I hadn't
so I went to look, and they were in a print that now that
I am older I realize was Miro, with the background dyed
chartreuse. They were very ugly and very modern and a
breeze billowed them out from the window. I stood in
the cool bedroom. My feet were bare and the floor felt
good. I wondered where Tom went with the steak. I
didn't think about the kissing I saw. I thought about the
green splotches on the bedspread. I picked up the
empty Grapette bottles and carried them to the kitchen
and Uncle Carl, who was so polite, thanked me and
suggested that I wash up and put on my pink dress because any minute our company would arrive and we
would serve the daiquiris and crackers and cream
cheese, and Jon was already crushing ice in the Waring
Blendor.

I went into the bathroom, which was the darkest,
coolest place in the house, and I washed the cat scratch
blood off my arm and changed into my dress and white
sandals, and next thing I knew the doorbell rang. I was
excited to see Max, Len, Dan, Alfred, Knox, Terry, Boris
and Bob; they said I looked pretty, and the smell was
aftershave and rum and the sounds were laughter and

Fat Girl

Edith Piaf and the Waring Blendor turning out more crushed ice.

Uncle Carl rushed into the kitchen to stick the green grapefruit under the broiler and then he rushed back into the living room and took into his arms the bouquet of flowers that Dan brought and said, "Welcome to our chartreuse evening." Everyone laughed and laughed and I knew this was a joke that was beyond me. There were so many jokes I didn't get and I knew right then and there that I would think about this evening for many years and I did and I have.

Early in August Mama and Grammy arrived in an ambulance, all the way from Missouri to Oklahoma. All Grammy's fat was gone and she mewed like a cat rather than said words. Uncle Carl and Mama set her up in an adjustable hospital bed in Carl's front bedroom. It was awful to see Grammy that way. Her dentures were out and her mouth folded in on itself. The temperatures were in the nineties and there was no air-conditioning. A tall fan was set up in Grammy's room, to blow on her.

Carl was teaching summer school. Mama sat days and Uncle Carl sat nights, next to the hospital bed. They washed Grammy's face with cool cloths and petted the back of her hands, which were black and blue from IV needles. They slipped ice chips between her chapped lips. They emptied the white bedpan in the bathroom toilet. All day and all night she whimpered. Mama would leave the bedroom and go sit in the living room and stare out the window. Uncle Carl did pretty much the same thing, except he also had to grade papers.

What I did was what I was told to do: I stayed out of the way. I walked to the pool and to the library, where they had air-conditioning, and that's how I spent days. Nights, after supper, I grabbed the cat for company, even though I wasn't fond of him, and I went to my room and listened to the radio. I liked it like that.

Uncle Carl's friends and neighbors and ladies from the Methodist church brought tuna casserole topped with potato chips and chicken pie and raspberry Jell-O with raspberries afloat in it and homemade yellow layer cake, off of which I picked the white mountain frosting. They brought flowers from their gardens. The next-door neighbor lady took away the stacked-up dirty laundry and brought it back clean. She even ironed my dresses.

I wasn't happy about Grammy dying and I still fifty years later dream awful dreams where I see her in the hospital bed and hear her whimper and scream and see blood cover her gown when she would throw up down the front of herself. I also wasn't happy to be living again with Mama. Uncle Carl was so busy with school and Grammy and his grief that he hardly stopped to say hello to me. Mama, when she wasn't caretaking, jerked me around and pulled at my braids and slapped me hard and told me how disgusted she was with me that I had been eating like a pig and was ten pounds fatter than when she gave me to Carl, which I was. She said that I was sassy and spoiled from Carl letting me run wild and do as I pleased while she had been in Missouri working her fingers to the bone. She called me "Sister Sue" and said I'd better watch it, because I needn't think that because we were at Carl's house that she would not whip the daylights out of me, although in fact she couldn't and wouldn't because Carl did not believe in beating children, and when she raised a hand to me when he was around, he'd say he didn't think it was necessary. She kept saying to me with a hateful look on her face, "Wait until we get home, Sister Sue. Just wait. You've got it coming."

After Labor Day Grammy surprised everyone by being alive. She sat up and she ate boiled chicken with the skin stripped away and the leg bone sticking out of the chicken leg. Mama had expected Grammy would be dead by then and that she and I would go back to New York. It had been a month Grammy and Mama had been there. Mama and Carl were not getting along. Mama told him she'd been carrying bedpans day and night and giving up the whole summer when she could have earned money while he went on about his life as if nothing happened. Those two could really fight.

Uncle Carl's best friend was Dan Huffman. Mr. Huffman—I called him that—taught piano at the same college where Uncle Carl taught. He was an extremely short, fat man and his round face was permanently flushed. Mr. Huffman couldn't drive but the man who lived with him, a veterinarian named Len Kimray, drove him. Len Kimray I was allowed to call Len, probably because he was a war veteran who had been out of vet school for ten years and was in his mid-thirties,

Judith Moore

whereas Mr. Huffman was in his sixties. Len was tall and slender and handsome. Every evening after Mama brought Grammy to Oklahoma, Mr. Huffman and Len visited. The first Dairy Queen had come to town and Mr. Huffman brought quarts of it, along with bakery angel food cake fragrant with almond extract, and we sat in the living room, which stunk of the cat and of my grandmother's cancer stench in the front bedroom, and we ate bowls of Dairy Queen with fresh peaches and cake or Dairy Queen and cake with chocolate sauce poured from top to bottom. We all stuffed ourselves, especially Mr. Huffman and me.

One evening when Mr. Huffman and Len came over Mr. Huffman got Mama to sing. At first she said, "No, no, no, I've hardly vocalized since Mother got sick." But Mr. Huffman settled himself at Carl's Steinway and Mama went and got her yellow Schirmer and gray Fischer scores. She began with Schubert's "Trout" and then she sang some murky, dark, dramatic Schubert song and the sweat poured off her in sheets, and then she wiped herself off and drank some watered iced tea that the ice had melted in and she sang "Un Bel Di." Her voice was clear and clean. As mean as she was, her voice was beautiful when she sang, and while she was singing I loved her.

Grammy kept on not dying, because you could not call what she did "living," and we stayed at Uncle Carl's. Mama enrolled me in school, which was across town by the Methodist church where Uncle Carl played the organ and Poe Williams and Raymond Fisher preached.

Fat Girl

Pretty soon, Poe Williams gave Mama the job as the choir director and we were going to stay a while.

We must have been very hard up. This was long before health insurance and the only person with a full-time job was Uncle Carl. I knew from hearing Uncle Carl and Mama on the telephone that they were trying to sell Grammy's house in Missouri but that nobody was making an offer.

When Carl or Mama told me to sit with Grammy so they could get something done, I did. What I saw in that room and what I smelled and what I heard was so horrible I cannot type it here. She clutched my hand with her hand, which was a claw. She had been so strong that she could kill a hog and move a cow into a stall. She had been so fat that she filled up her easy chair and poured out over her corset. As I stood by the side of the bed she whimpered "I hurt" and "I don't want to die." I never before felt anything so serious as what I felt when I sat with her.

When I started sixth grade I weighed maybe 150 pounds. Even after my mother got me new dresses, the sleeves sliced at my arms. For my first day I wore my favorite of my new dresses, a black watch plaid with a white pilgrim collar. I was scared when Uncle Carl dropped me off. Once I found my classroom I did right away what I always did when I was in a new situation with children my age. I looked to see if anyone was fatter than I was, or if there was anyone uglier. Usually at least one girl or boy was more grotesque in appearance than I was. But not this time. The girls were picture pretty, with full skirts that hit above the knee and blouses whose Peter Pan collars were starched and ironed. Some girls wore light Tangee lipstick and nylon stockings. These were the girls who already had little breasts. Their hair had been done, like Glenda did hers, in rags so that the curls came out soft and loose. Nobody was even chubby.

I was lucky that Glenda was in my same class. She made sure I did not sit alone at lunchtime. I think, even now, how amazing this was that she was so kind. Here she was, this popular cheerleader who got asked out on dates by seventh- and eighth-grade boys (but wasn't allowed to go) and she didn't ignore me. She introduced me to everyone and even her girlfriends were nice to me. None of those girls said one word about how fat I was or that I was dribbling sweat, although there were rough boys that Glenda said came in on the school bus from the country and they called me Fatso. Still, I hated the school and I hated the teacher. All I liked was lunch, where I unself-consciously, day after day, ate a bowl of kidney bean and hamburger chili and a plate of French fries and drank cold milk from a wax carton. Ketchup bottles were set on the table and I learned from other children, many of whom ate this same lunch, to pour ketchup into the chili and then dip my French fries into that ketchup pool. I could have sat there and eaten those fries and the chili and thick red ketchup all afternoon.

I could barely fit under the desk because of my

Fat Girl

stomach and sometimes, after lunch, in the hot class-room, I fell off to sleep. I already knew almost everything they were studying with the exception of Oklahoma his-tory. I could read French and conjugate French verbs. From going to museums on school outings I knew Pi-casso had a Blue Period and that Cézanne painted lots of apples and the same mountain.

I had for several years been reading grown-up books. They weren't necessarily good books, but they were books adults read. So this class and the work this teacher gave us seemed like work for children younger than I was. When you were through with a test or writ-ing assignment you were supposed to fold your hands and wait until the other children were through. I brought my own books to school, which mostly were books Uncle Carl got from Book of the Month Club, and when I was through with the class work I sneaked a few pages of my book and, as I said, sometimes I dozed off.

I think I dozed off because the air in the school-rooms was hot and still and because I was distressingly fat. One day the teacher came down the aisle with her ruler and slapped the tops of my hands hard and woke me up. I screamed and popped up straight and nearly turned over in this tight-fitting kiddy desk with me stuck in it and everybody laughed. The teacher told me I better straighten myself up. Boy, did I hate that woman, and from the sneer on her face when she looked at me, I'd say she disliked me too.

Carl and Mama were exhausted. They didn't have

money to hire what they called a "practical nurse." Carl's college wouldn't start until the end of September but Mama said she didn't know how she'd manage once he went back to school, if Grammy was still alive by then. Just Grammy's laundry alone took hours and the neighbor lady, a schoolteacher, had returned to her classroom. Uncle Carl and Mama were fighting a lot, hissing at each other, and then Mama would sit in the living room and sob. What I wanted to do was to stay out of that house as much as I could.

Glenda was busy with cheerleader practice and going places with her girlfriends. Not only was I a fatso supreme but I was a new girl with an accent that the Oklahomans said was "Yankee."

Nobody invited me anywhere and I don't blame them, and I couldn't invite anyone to Uncle Carl's house with Grammy dying.

But I didn't want to come home after school. So I walked, usually from three in the afternoon until suppertime. I went into cramped and dark mom-and-pop grocery stores and bought Fritos and a candy bar called Bit-O-Honey. Some afternoons I walked around the downtown and in and out of the Woolworth and the TG&Y variety store. Sometimes clerks thought I was a thief and they followed me up and down the aisles. But there was nothing I wanted. I walked past the two movie houses and the Carlton Hotel, where Mr. Carlton fell out of a third-story window and was in a wheelchair the rest of his life. I walked past the two-story building that had my paternal grandfather's name carved into a plaque bolted onto the building's front. This was the building where he had his real estate offices and where my father's brother had his law office. Although we shared the same last name and the same blood, that I might go in and introduce myself never occurred to me.

fourteen

"The female human being, given a certain
unseemly interpretation of her childhood,
specific to the absence of the male parent, will
tend to fixate on unavailable males."

—Carrie Fisher,
Surrender the Pink

The Methodist church was three blocks from school.
I considered getting an appointment with Reverend
Fisher. I wanted advice about what to do with myself. I
wanted advice about Grammy and my relatives in the
two-story building and about hell and heaven and
Mama's sobbing and about going back to New York and
about my mean teacher. I would go to his office and ask
him to help me. His office window looked down on the
alley behind the church and several times, while I tried
to amass sufficient courage to push open the heavy outside door and walk upstairs to the offices and ask for an

appointment, I walked up and down this alley. I never could make myself go in. I'd get as far as grabbing the doorknob and then I would turn around and trot fast down the alley.

Instead what I did was start walking the mile or so to Reverend Fisher's house. Glenda had showed me the Fishers' house, which was two streets from the two-story house where Glenda and her five brothers and sisters lived. This was a nice part of town, and although I didn't realize it, three blocks away was where I'd lived with my mother and father and the two houses where my father's mother and my father and my mother had grown up.

I must have known what I was going to do when I walked to that neighborhood, although, that first time, I didn't say to myself, "I am going to break into the assistant pastor's house and wander around." Where I got the idea to do this and the nerve, I cannot say. To do what I was about to do simply felt like the right thing to do next.

Nobody was at home at the Fishers' in the afternoon because, as I said, Mrs. Fisher was what then was called a career woman, and after the boys got out of their grade school a lady at church took care of them. The Fishers' house was on a corner. A high brown fence, taller than a tall grown-up, began at each side of the house and wrapped all the way around the back. There was a gate off the alley. The neighborhood was quiet.

Because it was early autumn and temperatures were in the eighties and nineties, sprinklers circled on lawns. I didn't see anybody driving on the street or walking on sidewalks. I went through the back gate and across the grass and up to the back door. No one in little towns locked doors and the Fishers' door squeakily opened right up.

I badly had to pee and I made right away for the bathroom and sat down on the toilet and peed. I wiped carefully and washed my hands. That done, I walked through the house, room by room. The house was dark and cool and still enough that I could hear the ceiling fan turn. The house smelled fresh and clean, of Pine-Sol and floor wax and bacon from that morning's breakfast.

I walked into the boys' rooms and looked at their toy boxes and bedspreads. Cowboys and Indians on horseback rode across the beige spreads. Framed in a gold frame, a mournful Jesus hung on the wall and gazed sadly down onto the beds.

I walked down the dimly lit hall and into Reverend and Mrs. Fisher's bedroom. Tables stood on either side of the bed, and on the tables were matching lamps. I knew which side of the bed Reverend Fisher slept on because his side was not the side with *Family Circle* magazines. On his side was a Bible. I ran my hand over his pillow. I opened the closet door and saw his suits hanging there without him in them. The closet smelled like aftershave and shoe polish.

I realize, typing about the Fishers' house, that this is a worse story than the story of what I did in June's apartment. This is lots worse. This is an almost-eleven-year-old doing a B&E, breaking and entering. Here I was this tub of a girl, long auburn pigtails dangling down my fat hunched shoulders. I wore huge dark dresses, and on my feet brown leather oxfords and white anklets. Underneath the dress I wore grown-woman sensible cotton underpants and a cotton slip. And there I was, wandering a family's home.

I stayed away from the living room, because it was at the front of the house and had a picture window. From the door into the kitchen I could see through that window and out onto the front lawn. I opened the refrigerator. I untwisted the lid on a glass container that held orange juice and drank straight from the bottle. I was, of course, hungry. I took out a package of bologna and a jar of mustard. I found the breadbox and the squishy Wonder Bread. I slipped out two slices of bread and with my index finger coated the bread with mustard, and between the mushy white slices I flopped two slices of bologna.

That was one of the best sandwiches I ever ate—the warm bread, the cold bologna, the sharp mustard. I ate it while I strolled the house, looking at this and at that.

On the kitchen counter sat a chocolate sheet cake, half gone. I carved away a slice and stuffed the chocolate into my bologna-tasting mouth. In a cabinet I found vanilla wafers. I grabbed a few and chewed them down to crumbs. I drank more orange juice. When I closed the refrigerator door the sound was loud.

I was scared the Fishers would come back and I was not scared. I hoped in a way that they would come back and find me and I would already be ensconced in their house as if I lived there. I could say Hi and they would say Hi and next thing I knew Reverend Fisher would call my mother and say that he and his wife were going to take me and raise me in a good Christian home. Mama would tell him what a bad child I was and he would assure her that he and his wife would manage whatever problems I had.

I also did not want to get caught in the Fishers' house. They would call Mama and Uncle Carl or the police and I would find myself in trouble that could lead to a girls' reformatory, which Mama threatened me with. But the real reason I did not want to get caught was that I wanted to keep coming back to their house. I wanted to make bologna sandwiches and drink orange juice and walk through the rooms and admire their house.

I wish that I could report here that I did not go back to the Fishers' house. But I did. While our teacher stood at her desk in our hot schoolroom and yammered about geography and history and simple algebra problems I counted down hours until I could slip through that back gate and across the lawn and into the Fishers' door. Some days on the counter there would be a chocolate layer cake packed with inches of rich chocolate frosting between layers and other days there were brownies or peanut butter cookies.

How many afternoons I visited the Fishers' house, I couldn't tell you. Certainly I went as many as ten times. I never stayed more than half an hour. I always made a sandwich, some days with bologna and others with pressed ham and American cheese (and I need to confess here that I never see or eat pressed ham without thinking of the Fishers and their house and my afternoons there and my crazy loneliness). I found a jar of sweet pickles and dipped down into the jar and took out warty little pickles.

One day there were deviled eggs. I love deviled eggs and I ate fewer of these than I wanted and then pushed the other six or seven eggs with their golden yolks, sprinkled with paprika, farther apart from each other on the plate. I always drank milk or orange juice or Welch's dark purple grape juice. We never had Welch's grape juice at our house.

When I was gone from the Fishers' house I missed the good smells and the peaceful quality of light in the rooms. I missed Reverend Fisher. I wanted something of his to carry with me. Two dressers stood in the Fishers' bedroom. One, obviously, belonged to Mrs. Fisher. Perfume bottles, a powder box, photographs of Reverend Fisher and herself on their wedding day and photographs of her holding the boys as babies lined the surface. A wooden cross sat atop the other dresser, and next to the cross Reverend Fisher tossed pennies and dimes and nickels.

On one corner were stacked ironed white handkerchiefs. That's what I wanted and that's what I decided to take. I reached for the top handkerchief and stuffed it into my pocket. I also thought a penny would be nice. I would call it my lucky penny and have it to stroke while I walked.

I had rummaged the Fisher house several times when I next went to Sunday school and church service in the morning and MYF and Sunday night services. When I opened the door into my Sunday school class, which was held in a classroom in the church basement, Mrs. Fisher smiled. She gave me a hug at the shoulders and I hugged her back because it was a cool morning and I was not perspiring. She smelled like her house. She asked how my grandmother was doing. She said that they prayed for her.

That night Reverend Fisher's sermon and altar call seemed more personal and he seemed, then, like family. His handkerchief lay folded in my purse, his penny sat in the patch pocket on the front of my circle skirt. When he mounted the pulpit and looked out at us, I gazed into his face and his eyes. He was on fire, he said, with the Lord. He wanted us to know Jesus as he knew Jesus. He wanted life to surprise us. I rubbed his penny. I smiled while he talked and at the end of the service when he asked us to come forward and be saved, I almost pushed my heavy self out of the pew and went toward Reverend Fisher's open arms. I wanted to be saved. I wanted to be lifted up.

Nobody lifts a fat girl. Also, no adult except perhaps a child molester will invite you to sit on his or her lap. I wanted to be lifted high up like I saw other children lifted. I wanted to sail in the air and be twirled. I imagined myself in Reverend Fisher's arms. He lifted me to his shoulder the way I saw the dads do with their children at the Macy's parade. What paradise, to be tossed into the air and caught. You could sprout wings. What paradise, too, to be carried, high above sidewalks and lawns and living room carpets, to have your feet never touch ground, to be airborne.

I was earthbound.

I wonder if the Fishers knew that for an entire Indian summer month, I haunted their house. When Mrs. Fisher pushed open the front door, ushering in first their two little boys, did she see the impression my bottom left when I sat on the cushion of a kitchen chair while I chewed a bologna sandwich and looked at *Life* magazine? Did Reverend Fisher realize that he was missing a handkerchief? Did I wash my milk glass and shine it enough with Mrs. Fisher's soft tea towel? Did the neighbors see me go in and come out? Did they describe me to the Fishers? Did they say, "She is a fat girl with long auburn braids. She walks hunched over. She looks irremediably sad."

You who are reading here may have an idea about why I lolled around June's apartment and ate her canned goods and about why I broke into the Fishers' ranch-style house and rather dangerously hung around and made afternoon snacks. I was hungry for love. I know that. But so are many sad hungry children and they don't rummage people's living quarters and eat their food.

How I managed not to get caught, I do not know.

*   *   *

One of the last times I sneaked in the Fishers' back door was on my eleventh birthday. I didn't stay long. I was afraid of my birthday that year and didn't want it. Every day life at home was worse. Grammy had shrunk down to white skin over bones and she hurt everywhere. No one knew why she had lived so long. She has a strong will is what Uncle Carl said. He and Mama were barely speaking. Mama's eyes were red and swollen. I didn't say much to anyone.

Soon after my birthday I woke up one night and heard commotion. Uniformed men were running out of the front door with Grammy on a gurney. Uncle Carl was going with them and Mama would follow in the car. "Get back to bed," she told me. I was awake the rest of the night, alone in the house, sitting on the couch and petting Tom.

She died that night, Grammy did. I was the only one who did not cry at the funeral. I didn't have any tears and I felt God was disgusted with me for not having a broken heart that Grammy died her agonizing death.

A few days after the funeral the hospital bed got returned to the hospital supply rental store. Mama scrubbed down the bedroom with Lysol. Scrubbing couldn't make the rotten meat smell of Grammy's cancerous flesh go away. Mama and Carl moved the double bed back into the room and they blew the fan into the room to try to air it out. So that's where Mama was sleeping and pretty much living, because she and Carl got on each other's nerves so badly that they avoided

Fat Girl

each other. Mama said that probably, before Christmas, we would go back to New York, but first Grammy's house had to sell and we had to get money.

Another thing that happened after Grammy died was the newspaper printed her obituary. My paternal grandfather and my father's brother and, I guess, the rest of that family read the obituary and learned that I was in town. Big Ham's wife, his third (by then the second wife, the one that was my father's first-grade schoolteacher, was dead from breast cancer), called my mother at Carl's house and invited me to my grandfather's house for Thanksgiving dinner.

Mama grabbed the fat on my upper arm and pushed me ahead of her into her room and told me that I had been invited. She said that it was up to me whether I went or not but that it would be disloyal, after all she'd done for me, for me to say yes. She said they were snooping, my father's family. She said for me to think about whether I wanted to go.

I said right away that I didn't. I really did not want to go. My father was a bad person and his family, no doubt, was bad too.

We were still at Uncle Carl's house when it got to be Thanksgiving. Uncle Carl, I don't know where he was, but we were not having the holiday meal with him. Maybe the noisy quarrels they were having, Mama and Carl, had gotten so bad that they couldn't spend Thanksgiving together. The only time they were polite to each other was when other people were around.

Mama said she and I were going to have our own

dinner. She made turkey breast sandwiches on white bread with lettuce leaves and mayonnaise. She cut carrot and celery sticks. She dropped the sandwiches and vegetables into a brown paper sack and told me to get on my coat and get in the Chrysler. It was a cold, dark day and the wind blew hard across the barren Oklahoma landscape. Winter had come. Why Mama was driving Uncle Carl's Chrysler New Yorker I don't know, but she was.

Mama drove us into the country. She parked along the side of a dirt road. She handed me my sandwich. She was still young, not even forty, perhaps not even thirty-five, and her wavy auburn hair hadn't begun to go gray and she was gorgeous. What she said was that I was being loyal by having Thanksgiving with her, that she had worked her fingers to the bone to raise me and that my father's family didn't care for me, they just wanted to get a look at me so they could report back to my worthless father.

The wind blew hard enough to shake even the Chrysler, and after a while Mama started up the engine and we drove away.

The day after Christmas we boarded the train for New York. By the time we got back to our apartment we had been gone half a year. I walked from room to room and there were no smells. After a few days I smelled my mother's face powder, her visitor, the stale sweat on her clothes. I felt put back in a cage. Mama pulled at my pigtails and kicked at my shins when I didn't hurry up or didn't mind her or when I sassed her.

Mama said this was it, this was the final straw how fat I was. I would be going on the strictest diet ever. By then I was eleven and I had been on many diets. I ate only what was on my plan. I knew the calorie count on everything, because it was in the back of Mama's cookbook. By then I believed that I was fated to be fat and smelly and dribbling sweat, that I could not lose weight and keep it off. No number of times that I ran around blocks, no swimming up and down the school's aquamarine pool took away and kept off significant numbers of pounds.

I had begun, again, to play with myself, something I'd not done for several years, and sometimes when I did, I thought of Fred in his buffalo plaid jacket, and this thought either made me play with myself more or stop playing with myself. I worried and worried that I would end up like the crazy boy back in Arkansas who rode the white horse, the one Grammy had warned me about. I thought about the white horse and played with myself more. I thought that any day I might go to hell or get put in the hot seat. I thought if for no other reason I might go to hell because I ate June's food and prowled the Fishers' house and never loved my grandmother, and now she had died a terrible death and I did nothing to comfort her in the way that Jesus would.

I think that this worry about Grammy and this playing with myself and my worry about it and my sweat and stinking, plus the fat I couldn't get rid of, plus my making Mama so mad that she took after me with the belt were part of why I longed so hard to toss myself out my fifth-floor bedroom window. I was stuck behind my walls of fat and I could not, no matter what I did, climb over. If I climbed out on the wide slate windowsill and threw myself down, if I flew past one after another apartment window, down to the concrete, I could split open my fat house and my soul would squeeze itself out of me and float to heaven on wide white wings where Jesus sat on his chair and suffered little children.

fifteen

"What you know about me now irrevocably binds us."

—Amy Gerstler, "Autobiography,"
Nerve Storm

After a few more years, we left New York and moved to northern Florida, where I would go to high school and where my mother would acquire a Ph.D. I began to get what Mama called my womanhood. The pubic hair between my legs and the hair under my arms ruined my life is what I felt. The breasts ruined my life. I felt ugly and more noticed. The odors were awful.

My period started. Menstrual blood leaked over the edges of the coarse pads and stained my nightie with blood that wouldn't come out completely even when I soaped the cloth with rough Lava soap and scrubbed the stained cloth hard between my hands. Not a day when I was bleeding did I not worry that blood would spot the back of my skirt, that blood would run down the inside of my cottage cheese thighs. I slept on my stomach because I worried I'd get blood on the sheets and Mama would scream. Soon after my period started, my mother took me to a beauty parlor and had my pigtails cut. The hairdresser, because I have naturally curly hair, gave me a poodle cut. The poodle cut made my hair stand around my face in unmanageable curls. I have the pigtails in a brown paper sack in the downstairs linen closet. Sometimes I take out one of the braids and smell it.

I did not want to be a woman. I did not want to be a man. I considered myself more animal than human, more rock than animal. I was a heavy piece of dull rock that bled onto itself every month.

The rock feels nothing. No matter what you do to it, no matter how many times you kick it, or how loud you laugh at it, or what filthy words you write on its surface or if you lie about it and say awful things about it that are not true, the rock does not care. The rock does not hear you. The rock does not feel you. The rock sees you dimly and not well. You cannot murder the rock. You cannot wring out its soul as if its soul were no more than a dirty dishrag you'd used to wipe up blood off the bathroom floor. The rock has a soul but its soul is small and looks like mercury and moves like mercury and does not exist in time as we know it.

The rock exists in slow time. One minute to a chunk

Fat Girl

of dull rock is one hundred years to you and to me. The rock does not weep. The rock bakes in the sun. The rock gets hot to the touch, too hot sometimes to touch. The rock does not buy a candy bar to eat on the way home from school. The rock does not go to school. The rock sits wedged into the hillside. The rock waits. It you sit on it, the rock does not give way. You cannot knock the air out of it because it has no air and no lungs and no stomach and no heart. It is good to be a rock, or, it is not bad to be a rock.

So, there I was in this Florida high school. I was bedazzled. I couldn't keep my eyes off cheerleaders and homecoming and May queens and princesses, with their straight hair and open-wide eyes and Bambi eyelashes. I studied these girls and their beauty in more detail than would have any teen boy. I imagined them slipping into their cheerleader skirts. I imagined their dainty Orlon panties, trimmed in lace, and their Maidenform brassieres, the cups embroidered with white satin stitches, the tab between the two breasts decorated with a white bow. I imagined their flat stomachs, the fine hairs on the flesh barely discernible in a good light, each hair not even as long as an apostrophe here that makes a word possessive. I admired the deep belly buttons.

I did not think of the dark patch under the panties. I was not interested in their sex or their musk or in kissing them the way that boyfriends kissed them. I was interested in and intrigued and flabbergasted by their beauty. They were gorgeous. They wore white Ship 'n Shore sleeveless blouses that showed off their tanned, lean arms. When they lifted an arm and revealed the perfectly shaved and entirely dry underarm, I was ecstatic. These pale underarms, some with oval shadows of dark shaved-away hair, were, to me, as lovely as great art. What care had been given these small, intimate patches of skin—the soaping, shaving, smoothing, deodorizing, powdering. I never wore sleeveless garments; my arms were too fat. And even in the long- and short-sleeved blouses and dresses that I did wear, I never lifted my arms. When I walked or sat at my desk or the lunch table, I kept my arms pressed hard against my fat-padded rib cage. I never raised my hand to ask permission to go to the bathroom or to offer to answer a teacher's question. I feared exposure of the huge wet circles of sweat that formed on my sleeves.

I thumbed through *Seventeen* magazine for hints on how I might make myself more like the girls on the slick pages and the popular, vivacious girls who brightened my high school. I knew though, deep down in my fat belly, that I would never be a May queen or cheerleader or *Seventeen* girl. I would wear no crowns. Who can tell of the envy of the homely young for their more glamorous peers? I pictured our cheerleaders as they jumped up and down in the cold Friday night football games, their long legs gleaming in the lights from the field, their heads thrown back and their perfect hair flying. I knew the cheerleaders' names. I did not go to the games. I sat in my room and on the radio I listened to the play-by-play, little of which I understood, and the halftime show.

In high school I was heavyset, but never obese. I was fleshy and flabby and homely and clumsy. My curls still stood around my head and no matter how many magazines I studied, I could not figure out makeup. Other girls were fatter than I was; they were slow and bovine and looked half asleep. I didn't care that they were fatter than me; what broke my heart was that I was fat, fat, fat. I never saw these girls in anyone's company. They walked, eyes directed toward the wooden floors, from classroom to classroom. I never saw anyone speak to them. I never spoke to them.

Mama and I rarely spoke. Evenings, she stayed in her room and I stayed in mine. She suggested that I cease calling her "Mama" and address her as "Kathleen." I refused. She had quit beating me because I told one of her friends about the belt and showed him the welts on my legs from a fresh beating. He told her if she did it again he would call the police. Until I left for college, he kept an eye on her, always gauging her potential for future violence. But for all that she quit beating me with the belt, she did not cease keeping me aware of what an unattractive, deplorable, selfish shit I was, the person who had ruined her life. "Oh, what I might have done," she would say, "had it not been for the likes of you." Or, she would tell me what heaven it would have been to be mother to a child who loved her. She grinned an evil grin and announced that she was counting the days until I left home for college.

She was in love with a man—a gay painter—who was not in love with her. As would I in later years, Mama was making a fool of herself with a man. "He's so sensitive, Max is," she'd say about this man. Uncle Carl remained at his job in Oklahoma—teaching students to play Bach on the college's aging pipe organs. He visited us in summers and spent Christmases with us and I never did not love him.

The summer before I went off to college I lived on salami and tomatoes and Pall Malls and I lost twenty pounds. I wasn't hoggishly fat. So I was thrilled when during the first month at college a fellow named Paul began to pay attention to me.

I was sixteen going on seventeen, just out of high school. (How I got out of high school a year early was by taking a series of examinations that proved I was ready to do college work.) Paul was twenty-one and a junior. He was a journalism major and junior class editor of the campus newspaper. How we met was that he sat next to me in geology, a choice made by alphabetical seating. Paul's long legs splayed out into the aisle. He wore brown cords and a loden green crewneck sweater (the colors, he would later tell me, were chosen by his mother to set off his red hair and freckles). His hands were freckled and his grin showed his teeth, stained by tobacco smoke.

Paul invited me for coffee. By the time he walked me

Fat Girl

back to my dorm, where freshmen girls weren't allowed out weeknights after eight and had to be back by midnight on weekends, I was in love.

There was another coffee date and then a Friday night movie. By that first weekend we were necking and necking led to touching breasts and that soon led to his putting my hand on his penis. His putting my hand on his penis led to his putting my mouth on his penis. Until Paul, I had never seen a penis. Not that he forced me.

By early November Paul and I were meeting almost every day in mid-afternoon in the student union coffee shop. We went out on weekend nights. Across the hall the university newspaper had offices. One Friday afternoon Paul invited me to his cubicle in those offices. The cubicles were created by movable partitions.

Paul's cubicle had in it a drafting table, a high stool, a desk on which he kept his green Olivetti. He sat on the stool and pulled out his penis and asked me to do him and I did. He ejaculated, then handed me his handkerchief. Wiping off my mouth I happened to turn my head and saw three of the paper's male editors watching through an opening between the movable partitions.

Paul did nothing. No, that is not true. Paul laughed.

I never spoke to Paul again. I left that school at the end of spring term and never went back.

Men like Paul, though, were the kind of men with whom I continued to involve myself. I was overweight, unshapely, awkward, homely and half nuts. Nobody nice was going to ask me out. Even when I was no more than, say, ten pounds overweight, I was not a girl a fel-

Judith Moore

low wanted to take home to his mother. There was something wrong with me that was more than being fat.

I fell in love, hard, with a fellow named Sam. I met him through the Episcopal parish of which I was a member. He was older by a few years than I was and he'd taken me out several times, in the afternoon, for iced tea. We talked, primarily, about books and theology. No kisses, though, no "I think I love you." I might as well have been a guy for all the romantic interest Sam showed in me.

I thought if I lost weight he might fall for me. I starved. Every time I wanted food, I pictured Sam taking me into his arms and kissing me on the lips and saying, "You are so lovely." I pictured the wedding—my white train floated on forever and Sam's dark morning coat smelled of mothballs and cedar. I pictured our Paris honeymoon, our first house, our two children. For several months I ate maybe 900 calories a day and I walked and walked and rode my bike. I took off another twenty pounds. I was finally slender, awkward, homely and half nuts and Sam didn't love me any more thin than he'd loved me chubby. Nothing came of this except that for ten years, off and on, I pined after Sam. He was the nicest man I'd ever had anything to do with. He was too nice for me.

Eighteen months after my freshman year in college I got married. My husband—Bill—was a decade older than I was. He was a graduate student in philosophy and a follower of Hegel. He was divorced and father of a four-year-old girl. He was brown-eyed and handsome.

187

Fat Girl

He's dead now and I will never know why he married me. I will also never know why I married him.

Six months after Bill and I married, I fainted on the way home from final exams at the University of Oklahoma. I was pregnant. I was eighteen, married, and we were going to have a baby, and Bill said it was time for me to meet my father, whom I hadn't seen since I was four.

At the university library, Bill looked up my father in the American Bar Association directory. He had a law practice in a small Illinois town. Bill dialed his office, introduced himself, and invited my father to visit. My father said, "Of course, of course." It was simple as that.

My mother, at this time, lived forty miles from us, and Uncle Carl, sixty miles. Occasionally, Carl drove over with my mother to visit. I begged Bill not to let it slip to my mother that my father was coming. She warned me all my life that nothing would be as disloyal as to have anything to do with my father.

I wasn't showing yet when my father arrived but I wore a maternity top anyway. I wore a black maternity skirt. Nothing else fit. We met him at the train depot. I was sick to my stomach. I didn't want to meet him. On that Saturday morning when he stepped down out of the sleeper car I looked away. Bill did the handshaking. I reached up and gave him an abstemious kiss. We drove him to his hotel in our broken-down 1947 Buick, whose front passenger door was held together with baling wire. He and I were to have lunch and spend the day together, Bill was to meet us for dinner.

Bill accompanied my father and me and the bellhop to my father's suite and then said good-bye. Once the door shut and I was alone with my father, I went to sit, uneasily, on a straight chair. My father sat on a long couch. We were across the room from each other. I allowed myself to look at him. He wore a dark suit, white shirt, a silk paisley tie. He was vastly obese, as overblown as a Macy's Thanksgiving Day Parade balloon. I looked like him, in the face. He began to weep.

I said I thought maybe I was going to vomit and took from my purse the bottle of Cola Syrup that my obstetrician gave me to sip when I felt nauseated. I drank down several gulps and fled into the bathroom, where I wet a washcloth in cold water. I sat on the closed toilet seat with the cloth pressed against my forehead. What went through my mind? I don't remember. I know that my father knocked on the bathroom door and asked if I was okay and said that he was ordering lunch to be brought up to his suite. Would I like a shrimp cocktail? he asked.

I came out of the bathroom. My father asked me to sit next to him and I did, although I did not want to. He had removed his suit coat. His white shirt was sweat-spotted. He was no longer crying but his eyes were red and he swiped at his vast perspiring brow with a white handkerchief. His hands, like mine, were small for his body.

A while later a waiter rolled in a heap of huge

Fat Girl

shrimp. The shrimp were piled atop a hill of crushed ice. Lemon wedges surrounded the ice. There was cocktail sauce and there were rolls and butter. My father and I ate the shrimp. The pink tails piled up around the bowl of cocktail sauce.

Once the shrimp and rolls were eaten, my father asked me to sit closer. I moved a few inches in his direction. "Closer," he said.

"Too hot," I told him. I felt like I was on a date with someone who liked me more than I liked him.

While we sipped Dr Pepper, my father in his deep basso voice told me about his life, from birth until the present. He got the LLD at the University of Chicago. He wrote textbooks for the American Bar Association. He met the woman whom, eventually, he married. She had been a schoolteacher. Now she was a housewife. They lived on a farm in Illinois; his wife, an only child, inherited it from her parents. They grew soybeans and corn. They had a son who, then, was ten. He was their only child.

He brought photographs. He got up to take them from his suitcase. I said, "No, no, I don't want to look."

He asked if I had questions. I said no. What I wanted to ask him I did not ask him—Why did you desert me? Why didn't you visit?

After that Saturday he began to visit regularly. He typed a letter to me almost every day for the next quarter century. I never was able to love him the way daughters can love fathers. I wanted to love him. I answered his letters. I became affectionate. I was performing. I was an actress whose role was fond daughter. I felt almost nothing other than dismay and grief and loss and shame about what had gone on between us.

By the time my father got to me I had made up so many heroic fathers that no way could even the best dad match the men I fantasized. It was like what happened with my mother. By the time she returned to Grammy's farm to take me back to New York I had built so many kindly mothers in my mind that no actual mother could offer what my fantasized mothers offered. No lap was as warm and welcoming as laps I imagined. I had evoked so many make-believe dads, had turned so many movie stars and violin and art teachers and preachers into devoted fathers, that my real father, bloated and awkward and guilty and ashamed, didn't stand a chance.

For years I skirted the truth about my parents and me. They didn't love me. They didn't know how. When they split up, my mother didn't want me and my father didn't want me, or at least did not want me enough to ask if he might see me, or talk with me on a telephone or send me a birthday card. What I was was leftovers from a marriage gone bad. I liked to pretend that, deep down, my mother loved me, that beating me and pulling my hair was something odd that just happened to happen. I liked to pretend that my father for fourteen years never bothered to find out how I was because he was busy. I still prefer to think he was too busy. I do.

Fat Girl

My mother, of course, found out I had seen my father. Perhaps out of spite I told her. She was unsurprisingly furious. She called me disloyal, she wrung her hands and said she'd worked her fingers to the bone for me and I now repaid her by keeping company with a lazy no-good lout and pervert. We rarely saw each other, she and I, after that.

So there I was, married to Bill, the first of two men who would regret having married me. I wasn't easily affectionate. In bed, I never quite knew what to do with my hands. I sprawled out on the sheets and let happen what would happen. I was a lousy lay.

Both men ate heedlessly and gained little if any weight; Bill the philosopher rarely moved from his chair and the other, second husband, Jack, rode bikes, climbed mountains, skied, and paddled kayaks through dangerous white water. The first of my daughters, like her father, eats and eats and eats and never gains. She lolls about on sofas and food is never far from where she lolls. She can eat a pound of pork roast at one sitting, together with potato pancakes, fried apple rings, roasted root vegetables and Parker House rolls. The other, like me, seems to add a pound if she so much as strolls a grocery aisle, and she, unlike her sister, is always physically busy.

I will never again fall for a thin man. If I have one last fling, and I can't imagine that I will, I want a fat man. I don't mean some beer-bellied messy fellow heaving for his next breath. I'd like someone who stands at or over six feet, weighs 225, maybe 250. He's more square than round, with a bit of pout to his belly. Summers, fat men wear loose floriferous shirts printed with flowers and tropical fish and palm trees. The shirts hang loose outside their shorts. When you head for the beach, the fat man's baggy swimsuit falls to his knees. I love double-breasted pin-striped fat-man suits; the tailoring hides bellies and lets peek out the vast snowy shirtfront.

Their mouths are moist, like muzzles. They are as talkative as they are hungry. Late at night, with a fat man curled in your bed, you can talk unashamedly about hot corned beef on rye and warted dill pickles. You can compare gravies and legs of lamb and mint jellies. You can reminisce about gingerbreads and peach cobblers and lemon custard ice cream. You can discuss every brand of commercially made cookies.

A naked fat man likely is as embarrassed about his tummy as a naked fat woman is about hers. He won't feel disgusted. He forgives your fat and hopes that you forgive his.

With a fat man by my side, I would have someone with whom to go on a diet. I already see the chart on the wall where weight loss daily is penciled in. I already imagine the pounds we've lost and the warm moist hugs in which we've enfolded one another. I hear us, fantasizing what remarkable garments we can wear when there's twenty pounds less of us.

A fat man would appreciate that I turned myself into an excellent cook. That said, I didn't like to eat what I cooked. I still don't. I prefer other people's food.

Fat Girl

Nothing I cook creates a hankering in me. I can make chocolate pound cake or any number of lemon desserts and because I've made them, they don't interest me. I want other people's food. Eating what I cook is the same as talking to myself.

As for my fat, I worked hard to keep down my weight. After the birth of each of Bill the philosopher's and my two children, I starved off my pregnancy weight gain. Not until the beginning of the end of my first marriage, when my husband was making love with my best friend, did I put on significant weight. My daughters were in grade school. My squat burly body embarrassed them. I could see their disapproval, or sorrow, or embarrassment. None of the mothers of their friends was fat. Plus we were poor and I wore cheap dresses and chopped my hair with sewing scissors.

When I was a six- or seven- or ten-year-old girl, bulging out of my clothes, if you had stopped and said, "Let's talk," and if you had asked the right questions, you might have learned that, like many fat people, I was a person who had been starved. In my case, you might have learned that I was someone whose mother, for her own reasons, could not love me, and whose father, for his reasons, had gone far away. I was getting love any way I could. I was one of those three little pigs who built a house of fat to keep from the door the ravening wolf from whose long teeth dark blood dribbled. Had you been a particularly skillful questioner, you might have learned that mean children, my mother and dead grandmother and my absent father were not the only wolves.

Judith Moore

I became my own wolf. You would have watched me eat at my fingers, rip off cuticle and chew and smile. You might have said, "This little girl is eating herself alive." But you would not have thought me lovable. You would not have seen me as pretty. You would not have been willing to take me home and love me.

Would love have done me any good?

Love, I think, would not have made me thin. Plus, by the time I thought of "love" as an answer, it was too late for love. I was too fat for love. Even when I was slender, I was fat.

Terrible childhoods are difficult to write; I have been frank here. I have told you how it was and is with me. Reliving these moments, I made myself ill.

Nights, I dreamed bad dreams. Days, those dreams played in the background. I slogged upstairs and slogged down. I hardly left the house except to take out Lily the Dachshund. I ate out of cans—water-packed tuna and garbanzo beans and sodium-loaded tomato and chicken noodle soups. My ankles puffed from the salt. You should read the labels on those cans. You will be amazed at the amount of sodium in, say, Manhattan clam chowder.

I never turned suicidal and I never jumped up happy. As I recounted those boys in my second-grade class or my terror on weigh-in days or the beatings with the belt when my mother hissed, "I'm going to cut the blood out of you," I felt relief.

Among reasons people keep sad stories to themselves

is that they do not want anyone to feel sorry for them. I don't. I don't want you to feel sorry for me. I do not feel sorry for myself. I am what I am. I am glad I wrote this, and I am grateful—very grateful—that you kept me company while I did.

Thank you.